SEMANTICS

To Mark, Justin and Geoffrey

SEMANTICS

Second Edition

F. R. PALMER

Emeritus Professor of Linguistic Science
University of Reading

Published by the Press Syndicate of the University of Cambridge
The Pitt Building, Trumpington Street, Cambridge CB2 1RP
40 West 20th Street, New York, NY 10011–4211, USA
10 Stamford Road, Oakleigh, Melbourne 3166, Australia

First published 1976
Reprinted 1977, 1978, 1979
Second edition 1981
Reprinted 1982, 1983, 1984, 1986, 1988, 1990, 1991, 1993, 1995, 1997

British Library Cataloguing in Publication Data
Palmer, F. R.
Semantics. – 2nd ed.
1. Semantics
I. Title
412   P325   80-42318

(First edition ISBN 0 521 20927 7 hardback
ISBN 0 521 09999 4 paperback)

ISBN 0 521 23966 4 hardback
ISBN 0 521 28376 0 paperback

Transferred to digital printing 2001

CONTENTS

PREFACE

This book is based upon a series of lectures on Semantics given at the Linguistic Institute in the State University of New York, Buffalo in 1971. It became clear that there was no elementary yet wide ranging work suitable as a very first introduction to the subject either for the student or the interested layman. The aim of this book is to provide such an introductory outline.

PREFACE TO THE SECOND EDITION

In recent years there has been a greatly increased interest in semantics, with, inevitably, new ideas and new attitudes. Above all, a major work of scholarship, John Lyons' *Semantics*, has appeared. This new edition plans to take these into account without destroying the introductory nature of the book.

TYPOGRAPHICAL CONVENTIONS

1

INTRODUCTION

Semantics is the technical term used to refer to the study of meaning, and, since meaning is a part of language, semantics is a part of linguistics. Unfortunately, 'meaning' covers a variety of aspects of language, and there is no general agreement about the nature of meaning, what aspects of it may properly be included in semantics, or the way in which it should be described. This little book will try to show what topics are included in semantics and some of the ways in which they have been, or can be, handled, but because of the nature of the subject and the variety of views about it, it cannot hope to be more than an introductory survey.

1.1 *The terms* semantics *and* meaning

The term *semantics* is a recent addition to the English language. A detailed account of its history is to be found in Read (1948). Although there is one occurrence of *semantick* in the phrase *semantick philosophy* to mean 'divination' in the seventeenth century, *semantics* does not occur until it was introduced in a paper read to the American Philological Association in 1894 entitled 'Reflected meanings: a point in semantics'. The French term *sémantique* had been coined from the Greek in the previous year by M. Bréal. In both cases the term was not used simply to refer to meaning, but to its development – with what we shall later call 'historical semantics'. In 1900, however, there appeared Bréal's book *Semantics: studies in the science of meaning*; the French original had appeared three years earlier. This is a superb little book, now sadly neglected, but well worth reading. It is one of the earliest books on linguistics as we understand it today, in that it treated semantics as the 'science' of meaning, and that it was not primarily concerned with changes of meaning from a historical point of view (see 1.3).

Yet the term *semantics* did not catch on for some time. One of the most famous books on semantics is *The meaning of meaning* by C. K. Ogden & I. A. Richards, first published in 1923. *Semantics* does not occur in the main body of the book itself, but it appears in an appendix, which is itself a classic in the field, entitled *The problem of meaning in primitive languages*, written by the anthropologist Malinowski (1923).

Other terms besides *semantics* have been used. H. G. Wells in *The shape of things to come* speaks of the science of *significs*, but he says that it was lost sight of and not revived until the twenty-first century. SEMIOTICS (or, for some scholars, SEMIOLOGY) is in current use to refer to the theory of signs, or of signalling systems, in general. Language may, therefore, be seen as a semiotic system, but it is not certain that it is useful to treat linguistics as a branch of semiotics (see 1.2).

There is, unfortunately, a use of the terms *semantic* and *semantics* in popular language, especially in newspapers, that bears only a slight resemblance to our use. The terms are used to refer to the manipulation of language, mostly to mislead, by choosing the right word. Thus there were headlines in *The Guardian* in 1971: 'Semantic manoeuvres at the Pentagon' and 'Homelessness reduced to semantics'. The first of these headed an article in which it was suggested that the term *mobile manoeuvre* was being used to mean 'retreat', while in the second the point was rather that by using a very narrow definition of *homelessness* the authorities were able to suggest that the number of homeless was considerably reduced. There is a perfectly true story, too, of the strip-tease dancer who wrote to an eminent American linguist asking him to supply a word to replace *strip-tease* because of its 'wrong connotations'. 'I hope', she added, 'that the science of semantics can help the verbally unprivileged members of my profession.' The eminent linguist, knowing his classical languages, suggested *ecdysiast*.

The term *meaning* is, of course, much more familiar to us all. But the dictionary will suggest a number of different meanings of *meaning*, or, more correctly, of the verb *mean*, and Ogden & Richards were able to list no less than sixteen different meanings that have been favoured by 'reputable scholars'. It is no part of a book of this kind to investigate all these popular and scientific definitions of the term, nor to ask if all the meanings of *mean* and *meaning* have something in common. But a brief look at some of the common uses may be illuminating, for we can ask which, if any, of these comes close to the use of the terms that we need in semantics.

To begin with, we should not see a close link between the sense we require and the sense of 'intend' that we find in *I mean to be there tomorrow*. It is significant, perhaps, that we cannot, in this context, talk about 'my meaning', to refer to 'what I mean to do'. Nearer to the sense we need is that of *That cloud means thunder* or *A red light means 'Stop'*. For *means* here is used of signs, both natural and conventional, that indicate something that is happening or will happen, or something that has to be done. Nevertheless, there is a difference between these two examples. The traffic lights clearly belong to a communication system in which it is the convention that red means 'Stop', but the clouds do not belong to any such system, and while they may provide us with information, they can hardly be said to communicate. Language is more like the traffic lights, but the analogy is not very helpful because their communicative function is derived from language and, moreover, from a limited and specialised use of it.

The most relevant use of the terms for our purposes is found in such sentences as *What does 'calligraphy' mean? 'Calligraphy' means 'beautiful handwriting'*. The reply to such questions is in terms of other words that the speaker thinks the hearer can understand. This is, of course, characteristic of dictionaries. They provide definitions by suggesting words or phrases which, we are given to understand, have the 'same' meaning, though what is same-ness is a problem that

we shall not be able to escape (5.3). The extent to which
meaning is dealt with in terms of the equivalence of terms is
even more clearly brought out when we deal with foreign
languages. For if we are asked what *chat* means in French we
shall almost certainly reply *cat*. It is interesting to notice that
we would not ask what *cat* means in French, expecting the
reply *chat*. Instead, we have to say *What is the French for 'cat'?*
In stating meaning, then, we are obliged to produce a term
that is more familiar than the one whose meaning is being
questioned. We translate from obscure terms, technical
terms, or a foreign language into words that can be easily
understood. It is obvious, however, that this will not get us
very far in our study of meaning, for, though the principles
of dictionary-making may be relevant to our enquiries,
we are not solely, or chiefly, concerned with writing
dictionaries.

A different use of *meaning* is found in such sentences as 'It
wasn't what he said, but what he meant.' Lewis Carroll made
play with the difference between saying and meaning in
Alice's Adventures in Wonderland:

'Then you should say what you mean', the March
Hare went on.
'I do', Alice hastily replied; 'at least – at least I mean
what I say – that's the same thing, you know.'
'Not the same thing a bit', said the Hatter.

This is a curious use for, if our words have a meaning, how
can we fail to say what we mean, or, rather, how can the
words fail to mean what they mean? The answer is, of course,
that we wish to suggest that the words do not mean what they
might most obviously be thought to mean, that there is some
other meaning besides the 'literal' meaning of the words.
There are a number of quite different ways of achieving this.
We can quite simply use such features as intonation or even
perhaps non-linguistic signs such as a wink to indicate that
the words must not be taken literally. In this respect there is
one intonation tune in English that is particularly interesting

– the fall-rise, in which the intonation falls and rises on the 'accented' word in a sentence. For this tune expresses reservations; it says 'but . . .'. For instance, with *She's very clever* it may well 'say' (i.e. imply) that she is not very honest, or not very attractive, while with *I think so* it would suggest that I do not really know (whereas a different intonation would express confidence in my belief). Similarly I can say, with sarcasm, *That's very clever* to mean 'That's very stupid', and if I wink when I say *That's mine*, I probably intend to suggest that it is not (7.1). Secondly, much of what we say 'presupposes' a great deal. The classic example is *When did you stop beating your wife?* which presupposes that you beat her at one time without actually saying it. This, too, we shall have to discuss in detail later (7.4).

All in all, it seems that we shall not make much progress in the study of meaning by simply looking at common or even scholarly uses of the relevant terms. Rather we must attempt to see what meaning is, or should be, within the framework of an 'academic' or 'scientific' discipline. Semantics is a part of linguistics, the scientific study of language.

1.2 *Semantics and linguistics*

Let us now try to place semantics within linguistics and see what that implies. To begin with, we can assume that semantics is a component or level of linguistics of the same kind as phonetics or grammar. Moreover, nearly all linguists have, explicitly or implicitly, accepted a linguistic model in which semantics is at one 'end' and phonetics at the other, with grammar somewhere in the middle (though not necessarily that there are just these three levels). The plausibility of this is obvious enough. If language is regarded as an information system, or more strictly as a communication system, it will associate a message (the meaning) with a set of signs (the sounds of language or the symbols of the written text). The Swiss linguist, Ferdinand de Saussure (1916: 99 [1959: 67]); referred to these as the SIGNIFIER (*signifiant*) and the SIGNIFIED (*signifié*). (He, unfortunately, used the term SIGN to refer to the association of these two, but some of his more recent followers have, more reasonably, used it for the signifier alone.) Examples of communication systems, all of them no doubt much simpler than language, are numerous. We have already mentioned traffic lights. Some animals make noises to communicate. The gibbons, for instance, have a set of calls to indicate the discovery of food, danger, friendly interest, desire for company, and they have one call that is intended merely to establish position and so prevent the band from spreading too far apart (Hockett 1958: 572–3).

Although it is reasonable to see language as basically a communication system, we must not push the analogy with other systems too far, for several reasons. First, language does not always have a 'message' in any real sense, certainly not in the sense of a piece of information; part of its function is concerned with social relationships (3.5), though this is also true of the animal communication systems too. Secondly, in language both the 'signs' and the 'messages' (the signifiers and the signified) are themselves enormously complex and the relationship between them is of even greater complexity. For this reason it has been convincingly argued that human language differs in kind rather than in degree from other 'languages'. Thirdly, in language it is extremely difficult, perhaps even impossible, to specify precisely what the message is. In other communication systems there is no problem because the message can be independently identified in terms of language or, rather, of A language such as English, e.g. *Red means 'Stop'*. For language in general we have no such easy solution, for we cannot define meaning (the 'message') independently of language. We can only state one set of meanings in terms of another set, only describe language in terms of language.

I have suggested that linguistics is the 'scientific' study of language. A scientific study must be empirical; it must be possible, in some way, to test and verify the statements made within it. It is easy enough to apply this to phonetics, for we can observe what is happening – we can listen to a person speaking. We can, moreover, describe the operations of the vocal organs, or, with the aid of scientific instruments, can measure precisely the physical characteristics of the sounds that are emitted. But there is, unfortunately, no similar, simple way of dealing with semantics. It is not at all clear what constitutes evidence for a statement about meaning, and some of the theories that have laid most claim to being scientific have proved to be the most unsatisfactory. Precisely what is meant by 'scientific' or 'empirical' in the context of linguistic study is a matter of some debate.

A further difficulty with semantics is that meanings do not seem to be stable but to depend upon speakers, hearers and context. Yet if linguistics is scientific, it must be concerned not with specific instances, but with generalisations. For this reason it is generally assumed that a distinction can be made between the linguistic system and the use made of that system by speakers and hearers. There is no real conflict between the assumption that there are rules of the grammar of English and the recognition that much of our speech is ungrammatical because we make mistakes, we forget what we have already said, we break off, etc. Similarly, a man who has complete command of the sound system of English may fail to make important phonological distinctions when he is ill or drunk. There are, however, considerable difficulties in deciding what is in the system or even whether it can be completely divorced from its use. This point was made, though in a rather different conceptual framework, by de Saussure (1916: 30–2 [1959: 13–15]) in his distinction between LANGUAGE (*langue*) and SPEAKING (*parole*). This distinction reappeared in Chomsky (1965: 4) as COMPETENCE and PERFORMANCE. (Chomsky differs greatly from de Saussure on the nature of the linguistic system within language or competence, but the theoretical distinction is the same.) Both are concerned essentially, as are we, to exclude what is purely individual and accidental (speaking or performance), and to insist that the proper study of linguistics is language or competence. But for both de Saussure and Chomsky, language or competence is some kind of idealised system without any clear empirical basis.

We must ask whether a similar distinction is valid within semantics. It goes without saying that we cannot be concerned with purely individual, idiosyncratic, acts. We may recall Lewis Carroll once again (*Through the Looking-Glass*):

> 'When I use a word', Humpty Dumpty said in a rather scornful tone, 'it means what I choose it to mean – neither more nor less.'

An individual's meaning is not part of the general study of semantics. Of course, it is interesting or important for some purposes to see how and why an individual diverges from the normal pattern. This is necessary in the study of literature – the poet may well not 'mean' what you and I would mean. It is obviously important too in psychiatric studies where the individual is apparently unable to use his language in the same way as others. But it is important to realise that neither the literary nor the psychiatric studies of the individual would be possible without the generalised 'normal' patterns to make comparisons with.

Nevertheless we need to make a distinction between what would seem to be the usual meaning of a word or a sentence and the meaning it has in certain specific circumstances. This may be a matter of 'meaning' versus 'use', or, as some philosophers and linguists have suggested, between semantics and PRAGMATICS. But the most useful distinction, perhaps, is made by Lyons (1977: 643) in terms of SENTENCE MEANING, which is directly related to the grammatical and lexical features of a sentence, and UTTERANCE MEANING, which includes all 'secondary' aspects of meanings, especially those related to context. It is this distinction that allows us to 'say' one thing and mean another (2.5).

1.3 *Historical semantics*

There will be virtually no discussion in this book (except in this section) of historical semantics, the study of the change of meaning in time. Yet a great deal of work that has been done on semantics has been of a historical kind, and it was noted earlier that the term *semantics* was first used to refer to the development and change of meaning.

Certainly the study of the change of meaning can be fascinating. We can start by attempting to classify the kinds of change that occur. The great American linguist, Bloomfield (1933: 426–7), noted a number of types, each given a traditional name. These, together with an example and the earlier meaning, were:

Narrowing	*meat*	'food'
Widening	*bird*	'nestling'
Metaphor	*bitter*	'biting'
Metonymy (nearness in space or time)		
	jaw	'cheek'
Synecdoche (whole/part relation)		
	town	'fence'
	stove	'heated room'
Hyperbole (stronger to weaker meaning)		
	astound	'strike with thunder'
Litotes (weaker to stronger meaning)		
	kill	'torment'
Degeneration	*knave*	'boy'
Elevation	*knight*	'boy'

We shall also try to find reasons for the changes. Some are no more than fortuitous. The word *money* is related to Latin *moneo* 'warn' (cf. *admonish*), because money was made at Rome in the temple of the goddess Juno Moneta. The tanks of modern warfare are so called because of a security decision in the 1914–18 war to deceive the Germans into thinking that water-tanks were being despatched. Other changes arise from new needs. The word *car* was an obsolete poetic word for 'chariot', until the motor-car was invented. Most scientific words have acquired specialised meanings that have no close relationship to the non-scientific use; *mass* and *energy* in physics are not what they are to the layman. A cause of fast change is taboo – a word that is used for something unpleasant is replaced by another and that too is again replaced later. Thus English has had the terms *privy*, *W.C.*, *lavatory*, *toilet*, *bathroom*, etc., and, more recently, *loo*.

Historical change is properly an area of comparative and historical linguistics, or what is more commonly called COM-PARATIVE PHILOLOGY, which attempts both to reconstruct the history of languages and, via their history, to relate languages apparently coming from a common source or 'ancestor'. One of the aims of the subject is to establish 'sound laws', to show for instance the correlation of *p* in Romance languages with *f* in Germanic languages (this is an aspect of what is known as Grimm's Law). This can be illustrated in English where pairs of words come from Romance and Germanic, e.g. *paternal/father*, *pen/feather*, *piscatorial/fish*. But the establishment of sound laws depends on knowing that the words we compare are the 'same' in the sense that they can be supposed to have a common origin, and this can only be done on the basis of their meaning. This is obvious enough in the case of the examples above (remember that pens were originally quills). It is no surprise that we can relate *ewe* to Latin *ovis* 'sheep' and English *ovine*, or *acre* to Latin *ager* 'field' and *agriculture*. It may be more surprising (but only from the sound, not the meaning) that *cow* and *beef* are also related (though in a more complex way). Less likely in terms of meaning is the common origin of *guest* and *hostile*, until it is remembered that strangers might be treated either as friends or enemies. Generally the less obvious identifications of meaning are well supported by the evidence of sound laws. We find words that ought by the sound laws to be related, and then look for reasonable semantic relationships. Unhappily this is not possible with all groups of languages. In many parts of the world the language relationships are difficult to establish, largely because we have no ancient records. Thus speculation may take over. Attempts have been made to relate words from different African languages because of some phonetic similarity, with no sound laws, on the basis of the meanings 'day', 'sun', 'fire', and, similarly, 'sky', 'above', 'rain'. Unless the identification in terms of sound laws is convincing (and it is not), such identifications are not very persuasive.

Apart from the scientific study of the change of meaning, it is an obvious fact that people are interested in ETYMOLOGY, the discovery of earlier meanings of words (or, if we follow the etymology of *etymology*, the discovery of their 'true' meanings). Indeed dictionaries attempt to satisfy this interest by quoting at least the most recent origin of each word. Interest in etymology goes back for centuries. The first serious discussion is in Plato's *Cratylus*; many of the suggested etymologies there are preposterous, but a number of them are basically correct. Part of the difficulty for the layman is that words are often not what they seem. *Gooseberry* has nothing to do with geese, and *strawberry* is not directly connected with the use of straw to protect the fruit (though both *straw-* in *strawberry* and *straw* are from a common origin relating to strawberries strewing themselves and straw being strewn). But few would expect *hysterical* to be connected with the womb (in Greek), or for *lord* and *lady* to have anything to do with *loaf* (of bread).

Etymology for its own sake is of little importance, even if it has curiosity value, and there really should be no place for a smattering of it in dictionaries. The chief difficulty is that there can be no 'true' or 'original' meaning since human language stretches back too far. It is tempting, for instance, to say that *nice* REALLY means 'precise', as in *a nice distinction*. But a study of its history shows that it once meant 'silly' (Latin *nescius* 'ignorant'), and earlier it must have been related to *ne* 'not' and *sc-* probably meaning 'cut' as in *scissors* and *shears*. And before that? We cannot know. Clearly, then, no serious discussion of etymology is required here.

As I said at the beginning of this section, there will be no further discussion of historical semantics. This may be surprising, and perhaps even disappointing, to the reader who has been led to believe by popular books and by the practice of most dictionaries to think of meaning in terms of change of meaning. But linguists have generally come to accept the

distinction made explicit by de Saussure (1916: 117 [1959: 81])
between DIACHRONIC and SYNCHRONIC linguistics, the first
being concerned with language through time, the second
with language as it is, or as it was at a particular time.
Although there are some theoretical problems about drawing
a clear line between these two types of study, in practice it
can be drawn and a great deal of confusion can be avoided if
we are clear whether a linguistic statement is a synchronic or
diachronic one. For instance '*Ought* is the past tense of *owe*',
'*Dice* is the plural of *die*' are confused statements. As synchronic facts about modern English they are untrue; they
may be diachronically true – but in that case the verb should
be 'was' not 'is'.

Linguists have in recent years concentrated on the synchronic study of language. It can, moreover, be argued that
synchronic study must logically precede the diachronic
study, for we cannot study change in a language until we have
first established what the language was like at the time during
which it changed. So too in semantics we cannot deal with
change of meaning until we know what meaning is. Unfortunately, because they have no clear theory of semantics, some
scholars interested in historical change have indulged in
vague statements of the kind we considered earlier. This
alone, I feel, is sufficient reason for concentrating, in a book
of this size, on synchronic matters.

1.4 *Semantics in other disciplines*

Linguists are not the only scholars who have been interested
in semantics. The subject has also been of concern to philosophers, anthropologists and psychologists, and there is no
doubt that linguistics has gained a great deal from scholars in
all three disciplines. However, because their aims and interests are different from those of the linguist, their approach
to the subject and even their delimitation of it have often
been different. It would be difficult to state precisely what
these differences are, and it is more useful simply to consider
briefly a few of the topics that have been considered.

Some philosophers have suggested that many, if not all, philosophical problems can be solved by the study of 'ordinary language'. It is argued, for instance, that the problems of the nature of good and evil, of right and wrong, in moral philosophy can be dealt with by seeing the way in which such words as *good* are used. The problem of 'good', that is to say, is seen as the problem of the use of *good*. This is only of marginal interest to the linguist. Nevertheless, some of the work of such philosophers has had an impact upon linguistics, notably that of Austin with his proposals concerning performatives and speech acts (7.3), of Strawson on presupposition (7.4) and of Grice on implicatures (7.5).

An older and more traditional area of philosophy that has interested linguists is that of logic, and there will be a whole chapter (8) devoted to semantics and logic. The logicians' proposals have ranged from the comparatively simple syllogism of *All men are mortal, Socrates is a man, Therefore Socrates is mortal*, to highly complex logical syntax. But a word of warning is appropriate here. Logic makes use of concepts that are found in ordinary language, e.g. those of 'and' and 'or', and relies ultimately for its validity on what we judge to be logically correct. Nevertheless, logical systems are self-coherent and internally consistent models of an idealised kind similar to those of mathematics and are not directly based upon, and therefore cannot be invalidated by, observations of natural language. Consequently, the linguist should be suspicious of talk about the 'logical basis of natural language'. The logical systems of the logician are far neater and consistent than anything to be found in language. They do not form the basis of language, but are a highly idealised form of a few of its characteristics.

It is also worth mentioning the distinction between science and the philosophy of science. While the scientist may take for granted the validity of his assumptions, his methods and his conclusions, the philosopher of science may question the whole basis on which he works. Such a distinction ought to be valid in linguistics, if the subject is in any sense scientific.

Unfortunately, there is still so little general agreement, especially in semantics, about the aims and the precise nature of the subject, and about the models of description to be used, that much of the discussion is more philosophical than scientific. But the philosophical problems will not be solved in the abstract. It is the essential task of the linguist to make such empirical statements as he can with the techniques and models that he has available. Only then can we usefully turn to consider the theoretical basis of his work.

Anthropologists are concerned with language as an essential part of the cultural and behavioural patterns of the people they study. The linguist would be unwise to ignore the fact that language functions within such patterns, a point that was made very forcibly by Malinowski, whose proposals concerning CONTEXT OF SITUATION are discussed in 3.3. One specific area of anthropological research that has particularly interested students of semantics is that of kinship, for the varied and intricate kinship relations of many societies are revealed in the equally intricate semantic patterns of the kinship terminology (5.7).

The relation between psychology and linguistics is judged so important that it has given rise to a subject called PSYCHO-LINGUISTICS. Essentially the psychological approach to language lies in the attempt to understand how we process language both in its production and reception. Sadly, we are still very ignorant about many aspects of this, especially in relation to meaning. Nevertheless, it can be said that the role of meaning seems far more important, even in dealing with grammatical issues, than one would have guessed from reading most linguistic works on the subject. For instance, it has been noted that there are problems with understanding sentences in which there is 'self embedding' such as *The boy the man the woman loved saw ran away*, where *the woman loved* is embedded in *the man saw* and the resultant complex further embedded in *The boy ran away*. Yet it is much easier to interpret *The question the girl the dog bit answered was complex*. There is clearly no grammatical reason why one should be more difficult than the other, for the grammatical markers make it clear that their grammatical structures are the same. But in the second sentence we have the obvious semantic links of 'girl answering question', 'dog biting girl', 'question being complex' and the process of interpretation is, because of the semantics, very much easier. This strongly suggests that even when the grammar seems quite explicit we rely far more on the meaning to help us with the interpretation.

It is largely through the influence of certain psychologists that behaviourist analyses of meaning have been proposed. One example is to be found in the works of Morris, e.g. *Signs, language and behavior* (1946). In this book he is concerned with signs and what they denote or signify. Thus if a dog is trained to expect food when a buzzer goes, the food is 'denoted' by the buzzer (though if no food is provided it is not denoted but merely 'signified'). We shall return to discuss in detail this behaviourist approach to meaning later (3.4). It is sufficient here to note that Morris compares the dog/food example with a man who prevents a driver from going along a road where there has been a landslide. Here the man's words are the sign, the landslide what is denoted, and 'the condition of being a landslide at that place' what is signified. But it is very difficult to identify the use of the terms *sign, denote, signify* here with their use in the example of the dog and its food.

A very different, and less relevant, approach is found in a book entitled *The measurement of meaning* by Osgood, Suci & Tannenbaum (1957). They attempt to 'measure' the meaning of words such as *father* in terms of semantic 'space', this space being defined in terms of a twenty-questions-like quiz: 'Is it happy or sad?', 'Is it hard or soft?', 'Is it slow or fast?' The results are plotted on a grid. But clearly this tells us little about meaning in general. It may say something about 'emotive' or 'connotational' meaning (see 5.3) such that *politician* will rate low and *statesman* high on the good/bad scale, but that is all.

A more promising approach might at first sight be found in

an altogether different discipline, communication theory. In this theory we have several familiar concepts that are defined technically. The communication system carries INFORMATION and the system can be judged according to the efficiency with which it transmits the information. In particular an efficient system will have minimum REDUNDANCY (parts of the message that can be removed without removing any information) and minimum NOISE (anything at all that interferes with transmission). In language there is a great deal of redundancy and a lot of noise. A simple illustration of the redundancy in the written language is that if the bottom half of a line of print is covered the line can still be read. Noise may be just 'noise' in the usual sense, for that interferes with communication, but it can equally be loss of high frequencies on the telephone or radio, bad enunciation or bad handwriting or, in the example above, the covering of the bottom half of the line of print. In fact, there must be redundancy if a message can still be understood when there is noise. In semantics noise may consist of the discrepancies between the speaker's and the hearer's understanding – for this will interfere with the transmission of the information. But this theory will not help us a great deal with semantics, for information in the technical sense is not meaning. It is not the effectiveness of the transmission of information that concerns us in semantics, but precisely what that information is intended to be. The human speaker, unlike the communication system, does not merely transmit the message; he also creates it, and we cannot even begin to talk about information in this sense precisely because we cannot quantify or specify precisely what it is that is being 'transmitted'.

2

THE SCOPE OF SEMANTICS

In this chapter I shall attempt to clear the way for the consideration, in later chapters, of the various aspects of semantics, first, by discussing (and dismissing) two unsatisfactory views of semantics which, though prima facie plausible, provide no solution to semantic problems and, secondly, by attempting to set out some of the more important distinctions that have to be made.

2.1 *Naming*

In 1.2 it was suggested that language might be thought of as a communication system with on the one hand the signifier, on the other the signified. But a basic problem is to establish the nature and relationship of these two.

One of the oldest views, found in Plato's dialogue *Cratylus*, is that the signifier is a word in the language and the signified is the object in the world that it 'stands for', 'refers to' or 'denotes'. Words, that is to say, are 'names' or 'labels' for things.

This is, prima facie, an attractive view, for it seems that all languages have words or expressions like *John Smith*, *Paris*, *Wednesday*, the so-called proper nouns, whose function is precisely that of naming or labelling. The child learns many of his words by a process of naming. He is often given names of objects by his parents, and his first attempts at language will include saying 'Da da' when he sees his father, or producing names for a train, a bus, a cat, etc., on seeing the relevant objects in real life or in a book.

Before we proceed, two terminological points may be made. First, although here and elsewhere we have talked about words, we often need to talk about sequences of words, usually with a grammatical identity, whole noun phrases for instance. For these the term EXPRESSION will be used. Secondly, a useful distinction can be made between DENOTATION and REFERENCE (Lyons 1977: 206–9), the former being used to indicate the class of persons, things, etc., generally represented by the expression, the latter to indicate the actual persons, things, etc. being referred to by it in a particular context. Thus, *cow* will denote the class of all cows, but *that cow* will refer to a particular cow. Unfortunately, there is no consistency among scholars in the use of these terms (and even in this book, when the distinction between 'sense' and 'reference' (2.3) is made, the term 'reference' is not being used in a way that contrasts it with 'denotation').

There are, however, many difficulties with this naming view. To begin with it seems to apply only to nouns (or nominal expressions in general); indeed traditional grammar often defines the noun, as distinct from the adjective, verb, preposition, etc., as 'the name of a person or thing'. It is difficult, if not impossible, to extend the theory of naming to include these other parts of speech. It is possible, no doubt, to label colours, as is done in colour charts, and thus it may be that the colour words (adjectives) can be regarded as names. But this is not at all plausible for most of the other adjectives. Since the beginning of this section I have used the adjectives *attractive, relevant, useful, traditional, difficult* and *plausible*. How many of these could be used as a label to identify something that they denote? The point is even more obvious with verbs. It is virtually impossible to identify what is 'named' by a verb. Even if we take a verb like *run* and attempt to illustrate it with a boy running (either in a still or moving picture) there is no obvious way in which we can isolate the 'running' part of it. With a noun we can often draw a picture of the object that is denoted. But this is difficult, if not impossible, with verbs. For let us consider the verb *run* and an attempt to illustrate what it denotes with a picture of a boy running. There are two difficulties that arise (even if we have a moving picture). First, we are not presented separately with a boy and with 'running'. We need a fairly sophisticated method of separating the two. Secondly, even in so far as we can distinguish the boy and 'what he is doing', it is far more difficult to identify precisely what are the essential characteristics of what is denoted by the verb than what is denoted by the noun. For instance, does running involve only the movement of the feet or are the arms involved too? Does it necessarily involve a change of position? Is the speed relevant? Clearly there is not something that can easily be recognised and identified as 'running'. The problem is obviously even more difficult with *remember*, *like* or *see*. Similar considerations hold for prepositions (*up*, *under*) and conjunctions (*when*, *because*), while pronouns (*I*, *he*) raise even more severe problems, since they denote different things at different times (2.5, 3.5).

Can we, however, retain the theory of naming, but apply it to nouns alone? An obvious problem, to begin with, is that some nouns, e.g. *unicorn*, *goblin*, *fairy*, relate to creatures that do not exist; they do not, therefore, denote objects in the world. One way out of this difficulty is to distinguish two kinds of world, the real world and the world of fairy stories. But this is, of course, to admit that words are not just names of things, and it must involve some fairly sophisticated explanation of the way in which we can, by some kind of analogy, move from giving names to objects in the world to giving names to objects that do not exist. Such an explanation is possible, but such words are evidence of the fact that words are not simply names of the objects of our experience.

There are other nouns that, while not referring to imaginary items, do not refer to physical objects at all. Thus we cannot identify the objects to be named by *love*, *hate*, *inspiration*, *nonsense*. When the grammarians speak of nouns being names of things we can ask whether *love*, *hate*, etc., are things. If they are inclined to say 'Yes, but they are abstract things', it becomes clear that the only reason why they wish to call them things is that they have nouns corresponding to them. But then the whole definition is circular, since things are what are named by nouns (see 6.1).

Even where there are physical objects that are identifiable, it is by no means the case that the meaning of the relevant word or expression is the same as its denotation. One of the best-known examples to illustrate this point is that of *the evening star* and *the morning star* (see 8.4). These can hardly be said to have the same meaning, yet they denote a single object, the planet Venus. Similarly, we may recall Gilbert and Sullivan's *The Mikado* where the titles *First-Lord of the Treasury*, *Lord Chief Justice*, *Commander-in-Chief*, *Lord High Admiral*, *Master of the Buck-Hounds* and many others all refer to Pooh-Bah. This suggests that it was misleading to begin the discussion by bringing in proper nouns. For while these are used to refer to particular people, places, times, etc., it is debatable whether they have any denotation and they can hardly be said to have meaning. We would not normally ask *What does John Smith mean?* or *What is the meaning of Paris?*

Yet another difficulty is the fact that even if we restrict our attention to words that are linked with visible objects in the world around us, they often seem to denote a whole set of rather different objects. Chairs, for instance, come in all shapes and sizes, but precisely what is it that makes each one a chair rather than a settee or a stool? Often the dividing line between the items denoted by one word and those denoted by another is vague and there may be overlap. For when is a hill a hill and not a mountain? Or a stream a river? In the world of experience objects are not clearly grouped together ready, so to speak, to be labelled with a single word. This is a problem that has bothered philosophers from the time of Plato. There are two extreme, but clearly unhelpful, explanations. One is the 'realist' view that all things called by the same name have some common property – that there is some kind of reality that establishes what is a chair, a hill, a house. The second, the 'nominalist' view is that they have nothing in common but the name. The second view is obviously false because we do not use *chair* or *hill* for objects that are completely different – the objects so named have something in common. But the first view is no less invalid. For there are no clearly defined 'natural' classes of objects in the world around us, simply waiting for a label to be applied to them; part of the problem of semantics is to establish what classes there are. Even if there are no natural classes, it might be argued that there are 'universal' classes, classes common to all languages. But this is not so. The classification of objects in terms of the words used to denote them differs from language to language. If, for instance, we take the English words *stool*, *chair*, *arm-chair*, *couch*, *sofa*, we shall not find precise equivalents in other languages. The French word *fauteuil* might seem to be equivalent to English *arm-chair*, but whereas the presence of arms is probably an essential characteristic for *arm-chair*, this is not necessarily so for *fauteuil*. Similar considerations hold for *chest of drawers*, *sideboard*, *cupboard*, *wardrobe*, *tallboy*, etc. The colour systems of language appear to differ too (see 4.3), in spite of the apparently 'natural' system of the rainbow. The words of a language often reflect not so much the reality of the world, but the interests of the people who speak it. This is clear enough if we look at cultures different from our own. Malinowski (1923 [1949: 299–300]) noted that the Trobriand Islanders had names for the things that were useful to them in their daily life that did not correspond to words in English (see 3.3). Similarly, Boas (1911: 20) noted that Eskimo has four words for 'snow' – 'snow on the ground', 'falling snow', 'drifting snow' and 'snowdrift', while, according to Whorf (1956: 210), Hopi has only one word to denote a 'flier' – an aeroplane, an insect or a pilot. But even if we admit the relevance of culture, we can hardly accept that cultural reality is already categorised independently of language and ready, so to speak, to have its component parts labelled with words.

We can, unfortunately, be misled by scientific terminology for here we often find that there ARE natural classes. If we go to the zoo, we shall find that each creature has a particular name, and that no creature can be labelled in two different

ways, nor is there any overlap between the classes. A gorilla is
a gorilla, a lion a lion. The same is true, or very largely true,
of the names of insects, plants and even of chemical sub-
stances. But these scientific classifications are not typical of
everyday experience. Most of the things we see do not fall
strictly into one class or another. Moreover, we should not be
misled into thinking that we can and should tidy up our
terminology by seeking the advice of the scientist. Of course,
as literate and educated beings we will be influenced by
scientific knowledge and may well refrain from calling a
whale a fish or a bat a bird (though why could not *fish* simply
mean 'a creature that swims in the water' and *bird* 'a verte-
brate that flies'?). But we can go too far. Bloomfield (1933:
139) argued that *salt* could be clearly defined as sodium
chloride, or NaCl. He was wrong to do so. *Salt*, for ordinary
language, is the substance that appears on our tables. It is no
less salt if its chemical composition is not precisely that of the
chemists' definition. *Salt* for most of us belongs with pepper
and mustard, which do not lend themselves to any simple
scientific specification – and neither should *salt* in its everyday use. Ordinary language differs from scientific language
precisely in the fact that its terms are not clearly defined and
its classes not rigorously established.

One possible way out of all our difficulties is to say that
only SOME words actually denote objects – that children learn
SOME of them as labels. The others have a meaning that is
derived from the more basic use. This is in essence the
proposal of Russell (1940: 25, 66 [1962: 23, 63]) who suggested that there are two kinds of word, 'object word' and
'dictionary word'. Object words are learnt ostensibly, i.e. by
pointing at objects, while dictionary words have to be defined
in terms of the object words. The object words thus have
OSTENSIVE DEFINITIONS.

Yet much of what we have already said shows that this can
be no solution. For in order to understand an ostensive
definition we have to understand precisely what is being
pointed at. If I point to a chair and say 'This is a chair', it is

first of all necessary to realise that I am pointing to the whole object, not to one of its legs, or to the wood it is made of. That may be fairly easily established, but it is also necessary to know what are the characteristics of a chair if the definition is to be of any value. For someone who does not know already what a chair is may well assume from the ostensive definition that a stool or a settee is a chair. He might not even be sure whether the word *chair* applied equally to a table, since the ostensive definition does not even establish that we are pointing at a chair as something to be sat on, rather than as a piece of furniture. Pointing to an object itself involves the identification of the object, the specification of the qualities that make it a chair or a table. It requires a sophisticated understanding, perhaps even the understanding of the entire categorisation of the language concerned. As the philosopher Wittgenstein (1953: 16) commented, 'I must already be the master of a language to understand an ostensive definition.'

To return to the child, it is clear enough that he does not simply learn the names of things. For if he did he would be unable to handle all the complexities that we have been discussing. Above all, learning a language is not learning just 'This is a . . .'; even less is it saying 'book' whenever he sees a book. We shall not solve problems of semantics by looking at a child learning language, for an understanding of what he does raises precisely the same problems as those of understanding what adults do in their normal speech.

In this section we have talked mostly about the meaning of words. But we shall also have to discuss the meaning of sentences (Chapter 6). It is enough here to point out that a naming theory for sentences is no more satisfactory than one for words. We cannot directly relate the meaning of a sentence to things and events in the world. The strongest view which relates sentences to actual things and events, such that *There is a horse on the lawn* would be used only if there is a horse on the lawn, is obviously untenable, since we can tell lies or make mistakes (there may be no horse on the lawn). A weaker view is to see meaning in terms of the conditions under which a sentence would be true – the meaning of *There is a horse on the lawn* being thus stated in terms of 'truth conditions' involving a certain kind of animal being at a particular time on a specially prepared area of grass. This will be discussed in 8.5.

2.2 *Concepts*

The view we have just been criticising relates words and things directly. A more sophisticated and, at first sight, more plausible view is one that relates them through the mediation of concepts of the mind. This view in all its essentials has been held by some philosophers and linguists from ancient times right up to the present day. Two of the best-known versions are the 'sign' theory of de Saussure and the 'semiotic triangle' of Ogden & Richards.

According to de Saussure (see 1.2), as we have seen, the linguistic sign consists of a signifier and a signified; these are, however, more strictly a sound image and a concept, both linked by a psychological 'associative' bond. Both the noises we make, that is to say, and the objects of the world that we talk about are mirrored in some way by conceptual entities.

Ogden & Richards (1923 [1949: 11]) saw the relationship as a triangle (Figure 1). The 'symbol' is, of course, the linguistic element – the word, sentence, etc., and the 'referent' the object, etc., in the world of experience, while 'thought or reference' is concept. According to the theory there is no direct link between symbol and referent (between language and the world) – the link is via thought or reference, the concepts of our minds.

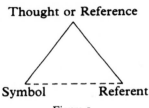

Thought or Reference

Symbol   Referent

Figure 1

This theory avoids many of the problems of naming – the classifications, for instance, need not be natural or universal, but merely conceptual. But it also raises a completely new problem of its own. For what precisely is the 'associative bond' of de Saussure or the link between Ogden & Richards' symbol and concept?

The most naive answer to the question is to say that it is a psychological one, that when we think of a name we think of the concept and vice versa, i.e. that meaning consists of our ability (and indeed our practice) of associating one with the other, of remembering that *chair* refers to the concept 'chair'. This view is totally unsatisfactory. It is not clear what exactly is meant by 'thinking of' a concept. Some scholars have actually suggested that we have some kind of image of a chair when we talk about chairs. But this is certainly false. I can visualise a chair in 'my mind's eye', but I do not do so every time I utter the word *chair*. If this were a necessary part of talking, it would be impossible to give a lecture on linguistics. For precisely what would I visualise? Moreover, if I have images when I think about linguistics, they will almost certainly be different from those of other people, especially my students! More reasonably, perhaps, what is meant is that I relate my utterance of the word *chair* to some more abstract concept. But that will not help either. For what is this abstract concept – what colour is this chair, what size or shape? In any case we ought not to be interested in what happens on each occasion, but with the more general question of the meaning of *chair*. As a phonetician, I should not be interested in the precise articulation of *chair* except as material for many more general statements of phonetics and phonology. Similarly, as a semanticist, I want to know about the general meaning of *chair*, not what I may or may not think every time I use the word. As we said earlier we are not concerned with particular meanings.

A more sophisticated version sees the link not as something we make every time we use a word, but as some kind of permanent association stored in the mind or in the brain. The difficulty with this view is that it really says nothing at all. For how can we, even in principle, establish what the concepts are? There is no obvious way in which we can look into our minds to recognise them, and still less a way in which we can look into the minds of others. In effect all this theory is doing is to set up, in some inaccessible place, entities that are BY DEFINITION mirror images of the words that they are supposed to explain. Wherever we have a word there will be a concept – and the concept will be the 'meaning of that word'. This is, obviously, a completely circular definition of meaning. It involves what is sometimes called a 'ghost-in-the-machine' argument. We wish to account for the working of a machine and present a total explanation in mechanical terms, but for some hypothetical person this is not enough – he cannot understand how this machine could work unless there is some kind of disembodied ghost or spirit inside it. Such an argument accounts for the phenomena by setting up an entity whose existence is justified solely as something that 'explains' the phenomena. Science has had many examples of this kind in its long history. Once scholars explained fire by positing the existence of the substance 'phlogiston'. Of course we can never disprove the existence of such entities. We can only point out that they explain nothing at all, and that, therefore, nothing is gained by arguing for them.

It is, perhaps, hardly necessary to point out that, as with naming, the sentence is no more satisfactorily defined in terms of concepts than the word. Neither the naive nor the more sophisticated version of the theory is at all helpful. Certainly when I say *There is a horse on the lawn* there is no reason to suggest that I actually 'think of' the concept, while a definition in terms of more abstract, timeless concepts is once again to say nothing at all but merely to interpret meaning by its mirror-image, postulated in an inaccessible place.

Although the philosophical tradition in the English-speaking world has been predominantly empiricist, there are many linguists who accept a conceptualist view of meaning.

This is part of a new mentalism in which a key claim is that intuition and introspection must play a large part in our investigation of language. It is a short and perhaps inevitable step to see meaning in terms of the mental entities called concepts. It is suggested, moreover, that if we are unhappy about postulating the existence of such wholly theoretical entities, we should look for a parallel in theoretical physics, which proposes that there are such unobservable entities as neutrons, and it is argued that there is no more reason to reject the existence of concepts than to reject the existence of neutrons.

This argument must be rejected for three reasons. First, the ghost-in-the-machine objection is overwhelming – nothing is said by moving meaning back one step to the brain or the mind. The position with neutrons is quite different. They are an essential part of the physicist's framework in that they are necessary for the predictive and explanatory power of his science. By postulating their existence he is able to account for quite specific observable data. But concepts do not explain or predict anything of this kind, and whatever can be said in terms of them can equally be said without them. Whether neutrons 'exist', when they are not three-dimensional entities, is a different and purely philosophical question and depends on the definition of existence, but concepts do not have even this claim to existence. Secondly, even if there were concepts in the mind they are in principle inaccessible to anyone but the individual, and we are left therefore with totally subjective views, since I can never know what your 'meanings' are. (Of course, if we had the knowledge to investigate the brain scientifically and could account fully for language in the structure of brain cells, both of these objections might be, thereby, overcome, but we are centuries away from such knowledge.) Thirdly, the arguments about intuition and introspection are irrelevant. We CAN introspect – and ask ourselves questions about our language without actually waiting for empirical data, actual recordings or texts. But in so doing we do not learn more

about our language or its structure; we merely produce for
ourselves some more examples of our language. What we do
NOT do by this process is establish the phonological or grammatical rules or structures; this comes from the investigation
and comparison of a great deal of data (even if those data are
all introspective). The same must be true of semantics, and it
follows that we should not believe that there are concepts that
can merely be discovered if we look in the right place. It is
perhaps worth considering that if scientists had continued to
rely on 'reason' (i.e. to look for answers to their problems
within themselves and their own rational processes) rather
than observation, we should still be searching for the philosopher's stone to turn lead into gold.

Finally, in this section it is worth noting that to some
extent DUALISM, the view of language described here and in
the previous section that sees meaning as part of the signified/
signifier relation, is encouraged by the term *meaning* itself
and by the statement that words (and sentences) HAVE meaning. For if this is so it is obviously legitimate to ask what
kind of entity meaning is, and to look for it either in the world
or in people's minds. But to say that a word has meaning
is not like saying that people have legs or that trees have
leaves. We are easily misled by the verb *have* and the fact
that *meaning* is a noun into looking for something that IS
meaning.

In practice we all know what it is for a word to have
meaning. Knowing the meaning of a word means that we can
do a number of things – we can use it properly, we can
explain it to others in terms of paraphrases or synonyms. But
it does not follow from that that there is an entity that IS
meaning or a whole group of entities that ARE the meaning of
words. For a word to mean something is similar in some way
to a notion that a signpost points somewhere; we can understand the meaning of a word just as we can read the signpost.
But it does not make sense to ask what it is that words mean
any more than to ask what it is that signposts point to. It is
not sense, that is to say, to ask IN GENERAL what words mean

or signposts point to. It is sense only to ask 'What does THIS word mean?', 'What does THIS signpost point to?'.

The problem of semantics is not, then, nor can it be, the search for an elusive entity called 'meaning'. It is rather an attempt to understand how it is that words and sentences can 'mean' at all, or better perhaps, how they can be meaningful. If we are talking of 'having' meaning, it is rather like talking about 'having' length. Having length is being so many feet or inches long; length is not something over and above this. Similarly, meaning is not some entity that words or any other linguistic entities 'have', in any literal sense of 'having'.

Wittgenstein (1953: 31) said 'for a large class of words . . . the meaning of a word is its use in the language'. This is not a very helpful remark since we are perhaps not much clearer about the 'use' of a word than we are about its meaning. But it has some value; we can investigate use, and we are less likely to think of use as something that words 'have' in any literal sense, and less likely to waste our time in an attempt to discover precisely what it is.

2.3 *Sense and reference*

The term REFERENCE has already been used to contrast with DENOTATION (2.1). It is also used in a useful, but wider sense, to contrast with SENSE, to distinguish between two very different, though related, aspects of meaning.

Reference deals with the relationship between the linguistic elements, words, sentences, etc., and the non-linguistic world of experience. Sense relates to the complex system of relationships that hold between the linguistic elements themselves (mostly the words); it is concerned only with intra-linguistic relations.

It might seem reasonable to argue that semantics is concerned only with the way we relate our language to our experience and so to say that reference is the essential element of semantics. Yet sense relationships have formed an important part of the study of language. For consider the words *ram* and *ewe*. These on the one hand refer to particular kinds of animals and derive their meaning in this way. But they also belong to a pattern in English that includes *cow/bull*, *sow/boar*, *mare/stallion*, etc. Older grammars of English treated this as a part of grammar, because it was clearly related to sex, and sex was supposedly a matter of gender (since sex and gender are related in some degree in Latin). But there are other kinds of related words, e.g. *duck/duckling*, *pig/piglet* (involving adult and young), or *father/son*, *uncle/nephew* (involving family relationships), and these are not usually thought to be grammatical. They are rather a part of the 'semantic structure' of English. There are many other kinds of sense relations, too, e.g. those exemplified by *narrow/wide*, *dead/alive*, *buy/sell*; these we shall discuss in some detail later. The dictionary is usually concerned with sense relations, with relating words to words, though most dictionaries state such relations in a most unsystematic way (Chapter 5). It could be argued, though, that the ultimate aim of the dictionary is to supply its user with referential meaning, and that it does so by relating, via sense relations, a word whose meaning is unknown to a word or words whose reference is already understood.

We have, then, two kinds of semantics, one that deals with semantic structure and the other that deals with meaning in terms of our experience outside language. But the situation should not surprise the linguist, since he has a similar situation at the other 'end' of his language model, where we had tentatively placed phonetics (1.2). For linguists distinguish between PHONETICS, which deals with speech sounds as such and describes them in terms of their auditory or acoustic characteristics or of the articulations of the vocal organs, and PHONOLOGY, which deals with the sound systems of languages in terms of the internal relations between sounds. But we should not push the analogy too far. It is enough to see that there may be two kinds of semantics, one that relates to non-linguistic entities, and one that is intra-linguistic.

We are not concerned, however, only with words but also with sentences. Indeed, most scholars who have dealt with sense have been primarily concerned with sentence meaning and its relation to word meaning. Bierwisch (1970: 167) argues that a semantic theory must explain such sentences as

(1)   *His typewriter has bad intentions.*
(2)   *My unmarried sister is married to a bachelor.*
(3)   *John was looking for the glasses.*
(4) (a) *The needle is too short.*
    (b) *The needle is not long enough.*
(5) (a) *Many of the students were unable to answer your question.*
    (b) *Only a few students grasped your question.*
(6) (a) *How long did Archibald remain in Monte Carlo?*
    (b) *Archibald remained in Monte Carlo for some time.*

(1) is an example of an anomalous sentence, (2) of a contradictory one and (3) of an ambiguous one; (4) illustrates paraphrase or synonymous sentences; in (5) one sentence follows from the other, while in (6) the first implies or presupposes the second.

In recent years some linguists have attempted to limit semantics, both in theory and in practice, to sense relations. One example is to be found in a well-known article (Katz & Fodor 1963: 176), where we read 'A semantic theory describes and explains the interpretive ability of speakers; by accounting for their performance in determining the number of readings of a sentence; by detecting semantic anomalies; by deciding upon paraphrase relations between sentences; and by marking every other semantic property or relation that plays a role in this ability.' Here there is explicit reference only to ambiguity ('the number of readings'), anomaly and paraphrase, but, in a later work, Katz (1972: 45, 47–54) lists no less than fifteen such relations. The speaker's ability does not, however, include his ability to relate the sentences to the world of experience, and indeed Katz & Fodor explicitly exclude from a semantic theory any reference to the settings of sentences. We shall discuss this view, in some detail, in 3.2.

It is not always possible to distinguish clearly between sense and reference for the simple reason that the categories of our language correspond, to some degree at least, to real-world distinctions. Whether language determines the shape of the world or vice versa (see 3.1) is probably a 'chicken and egg' problem. The fact that we have *ram/ewe*, *bull/cow* is part of the semantic structure of English, but it also relates to the fact that there are male and female sheep and cattle. But we have to remember (1) that not all languages will make the same distinctions, (2) that there is considerable indeterminacy in the categorisation of the real world – as we saw in our discussion of names, some things (e.g. the mammals) fall into fairly natural classes, others do not. It is because of this that we can distinguish sense and reference, yet must allow that there is no absolute line between them, between what is in the world and what is in language.

2.4 *The word*

Dictionaries appear to be concerned with stating the meanings of words and it is, therefore, reasonable to assume that the word is one of the basic units of semantics. Yet there are difficulties.

To begin with, not all words have the same kind of meaning as others; some seem to have little or none. In, for instance, *Boys like to play* it is easy enough to consider what might be the meaning of *boys*, *like* and *play*, but what is the meaning of *to*? It has been argued that meaning implies choice and that while we can replace *boys*, *like* and *play* by *girls*, *hate* and *fight*, *to* cannot be replaced by anything, but is wholly predictable in this environment, and so has no meaning at all. The nineteenth-century English grammarian, Henry Sweet (1891: 22) drew a distinction between 'full' words and 'form' words. Examples of full words are *tree*, *sing*, *blue*, *gently* and of form words *it*, *the*, *of*, *and*. It is only the full words that seem to have the kind of meaning that we would expect to find in a dictionary. The form words belong rather to the grammar and have only 'grammatical' meaning. Such meaning cannot be stated in isolation, but only in relation to other words and even sometimes to the whole sentence.

The word, moreover, is not a clearly defined linguistic unit. It is to some degree purely conventional, defined in terms of the spaces in the written text. Of course, this spacing is not wholly arbitrary, and there are several sound reasons why we make the divisions as we do. One signal in the spoken language is stress, in that one word seems to allow only one main stress, and we can, for that reason, treat *bláckbird* as a single word, but *bláck bírd* as two. But there is no complete correlation between the spoken and the written form, as evidenced by *The Whíte House*, or by compounds such as *shóeblack*, *shóe-horn* and *shóe polish*, all with a single stress. Bloomfield (1933: 178) offered a solution by suggesting that the word is the 'minimum free form', the smallest form that may occur in isolation. But this all depends on what is meant by 'in isolation'. For we shall not normally say *the*, *is*, *by* in isolation. We might, of course, produce these 'words' in reply to a question such as *What is the second word here?* or *Did you say 'a' or 'the'?* But this just begs the question. We learn to utter in isolation just those items that we have learnt to recognise as words.

Bloomfield also suggested that we should look for an element smaller than the word, a unit of meaning – the MORPHEME: examples are *-berry* in *blackberry* or *-y* in *Johnny*. Later linguists were more interested in the status of such words as *loved* where they could identify the morphemes *love-* and *-d*. Here the two elements seem clearly to have the distinct meanings of 'adore' and 'past'. But problems soon arose with words such as *took*, which appears to be both 'take' and 'past', yet cannot be segmented in any obvious way into two parts each with its own meaning. The best way to handle this is not in terms of morphemes (i.e. parts of words), but rather by redefining the term *word* in a different, though not unfamiliar way. We have been using this term in the sense that *love* and *loved* are different words. But we could also say that they are forms of the same word – the verb 'to love' (which, oddly enough, we identify by using two words, *to* and *love*). A technical term for the word in this second sense is LEXEME. It is lexemes that usually provide dictionary headings. There are not two entries for *love* and *loved*, but one only (and this may even include the noun *love* as well as the verb, though we may not wish to extend the term *lexeme* in a similar way). If we proceed on these lines we can talk about the meaning of words (i.e. lexemes), and independently of the meaning of grammatical elements such as plural or past tense. Instead of treating *loved* as the two morphemes *love-* and *-d*, we shall analyse it in terms of the lexeme *love* and the grammatical category of tense. This solution leaves us with the word (defined as the lexeme) as the unit for our dictionary, and completely avoids the problem of identifying the separate elements of *took*. But we are still left with the status of compounds (see 4.5).

Even if we can identify elements within the word without actually segmenting the word itself, there are still problems about stating the meaning of the elements. The grammatical elements, like the grammatical words we considered earlier, often seem to have little or no meaning. In some cases the meaning seems to be fairly simple and independent, e.g. 'more than one' for plural; yet even this is not entirely true, while gender is often only superficially related to sex (see 6.1). Other grammatical elements are almost devoid of any recognisable meaning, e.g. those of case in Latin, which for the most part simply indicate grammatical relations within the sentence – the subject, the object, etc. (6.4).

There are even some elements within words that are not grammatical yet equally have little or no meaning. Bloomfield was particularly concerned about the status of *cran-* in *cranberry*, which seems to have no independent meaning and does not occur in any other words. He might well have been concerned with *straw-* and *goose-* in *strawberry* and *gooseberry*, which have nothing to do with straw or geese. In contrast *black-* in *blackberry* can be related both in form and in meaning to the first elements of *blackbird* and *black-board*. An interesting trio is *greenfinch*, *bullfinch* and *chaffinch*. All are names of finches. In *greenfinch*, *green-* actually indicates its colour; in *bullfinch* the first element can be identified, but has little connection with bulls; while the first element of *chaffinch* seems to have no meaning at all. Even more striking is the fact that there are many words in English that are called PHONAESTHETIC, in which one part, often the initial cluster of consonants, gives an indication of meaning of a rather special kind. Thus many words beginning with *sl-* are 'slippery' in some way – *slide*, *slip*, *slither*, *slush*, *sluice*, *sludge*, etc., or else they are merely pejorative – *slattern*, *slut*, *slang*, *sly*, *sloppy*, *slovenly*, etc. The *sk-* words refer to surfaces or superficiality – *skate*, *skimp*, *skid*, *skim*, *skin*, etc. The reader may consider also the meaning of words beginning with *sn-*, *str-*, *sw-*, *tw-*, etc. An amusing set is that which ends in *-ump*; almost all refer to some kind of roundish mass – *plump*, *chump*, *rump*, *hump*, *lump*, *bump*, *stump*, and even perhaps *dump* and *mumps*. But we cannot generalise too far. Not every word with these phonological characteristics will have the meaning suggested, and, moreover, we cannot separate this part and state the meaning of the remainder, e.g. the meaning of *-ide* in *slide* or *-ate* in *skate*.

There is no consistency about the number of semantic units we may recognise within a word. Although we have *ram/ewe*, *stallion/mare*, we have no similar pairs for *giraffe* or *elephant*. We have to say *male giraffe*, *female giraffe*, or if we know the correct term *bull elephant* and *cow elephant*. Such considerations, together with the fact that we have the words *cow* and *calf*, may lead us to define *bull* as *male adult bovine animal* and to see this as an indication of four distinct elements of meaning in the same word. This point is related to the distinction made by Ullmann (1962: 8off.) between TRANSPARENT and OPAQUE words. Transparent words are those whose meaning can be determined from the meaning of their parts, opaque words those for which this is not possible. Thus *chopper* and *doorman* are transparent, but *axe* and *porter* are opaque. Comparison with other languages, German in particular, is interesting. In English *thimble, glove* and *linguistics* are opaque (the same is true of the equivalent French words, too); in German the corresponding words are all transparent – *Fingerhut* ('finger-hat'), *Handschuh* ('hand-shoe'), *Sprachwissenschaft* ('language-science'). But there are degrees of transparency and opacity. A chopper may indeed be an instrument that chops, but does a screwdriver actually DRIVE screws? What are we to say of *spanner* and *hammer*? The *-er* ending looks as if it is the indication of an instrument, but a spanner spans only in a now obsolete sense of *span* ('wind up'), while a hammer does not 'ham' at all. Similar comments can be made about the *-berry* and *-finch* words that we considered earlier. We can, then, hardly use transparent words to decide what are the semantic elements within opaque ones; we should not wish to argue for the analysis of *thimble* on the basis of *Fingerhut*.

Finally, we must notice that some whole groups of words must be taken together to establish meaning. These are IDIOMS – sequences of words whose meaning cannot be predicted from the meanings of the words themselves. Familiar examples are *kick the bucket, fly off the handle, spill the beans, red herring*. The point is clear if we contrast *kick the table, fly off the roof, spill the coffee, red fish*. Semantically, idioms are single units, but they are not single grammatical units like words, for there is no past tense **kick the bucketed*. There will be a more detailed discussion in 4.5.

Sometimes semantic division seems to 'override' word division. Consider, for example, *heavy smoker* and *good singer*. Semantically these are not *heavy* + *smoker* (a smoker who is heavy) and *good* + *singer* (a singer who is good). The meaning rather is one who smokes heavily or sings well. We can divide, if we insist, but the first division would have to be between *heavy smok-* and *-er, good sing-* and *-er*, if we want to retain the parallelism between the form and the meaning. An alternative solution would be in terms of DEEP STRUCTURE, which would allow the statement of the meaning of *heavy* *smoker* in terms of *X smokes heavily* (see 6.1). But this might not be so easy with some other rather amusing examples that have been suggested – *artificial florist* and *criminal lawyer*.

All these considerations may suggest that we should abandon the idea that the word is a natural unit for semantics, however useful it may be for the dictionary maker. Bazell (1954 [1966: 339]) commented, 'To seek a semantic unit within the boundaries of the word simply because these boundaries are clearer than others is like looking for a lost ball on the lawn simply because the thicket provides poor ground for such a search.' But we cannot proceed without some kind of lexical unit and the lexeme seems the most obvious one, even if its definition may on occasions be arbitrary, and if the meaning of sequences of words is not always (wholly) predictable from the lexemes contained in them.

2.5 *The sentence*

Apart from all the problems concerning the word itself, there is the question whether the basic unit of meaning is not the word after all, but the sentence. For it is, surely, with sentences that we communicate, and this is reflected in the traditional definition of the sentence as 'the expression of a complete thought'. If words have meaning, it could be argued, it is derived from their function as parts of sentences. Even if referential meaning is established by ostensive definition, such definition is achieved only by sentences of the kind *This is a* . . ., and such meaning, therefore, is ultimately statable only in terms of the sentence.

The sentence is essentially a grammatical unit; indeed it is the function of syntax to describe the structure of the sentence and thereby to define it. English sentences will consist minimally of a subject noun phrase and a verb phrase as its predicate or complement. Each of these may be a single word as in *Birds fly*. The syntax will determine much more complex structures than this, of course. However, we do not always produce complete sentences even of this minimal kind. It is simple enough to envisage a situation in which someone might simply say *Horses*. This could be in reply to a question such as *What are those animals in that field?* Although some scholars have talked of 'one word sentences' in describing such expressions, it seems more helpful to treat *Horses* as a sentence fragment and as an incomplete version of *They are horses*; certainly we should need to reconstruct the complete sentence in this way to talk about its meaning. Most fragments are closely linked to their linguistic context and handled in terms of ellipsis (the omission of parts of the sentences). Ellipsis in turn is related to the feature of 'pro-formation' (the use of pronouns and similar forms that replace verbs and other parts of speech). All are devices for not repeating everything that has already been established in the discourse. Thus, in *John saw Mary and spoke to her*, *John* is omitted, while *Mary* is replaced by *her* in the second half of the sentence. Not all sentence fragments, however, are linked to the previous discourse. *Coming?* or *Coming!* may be used instead of *Are you coming?* or *I'm coming!* Moreover, in actual speech we often fail simply through lapse of memory or inattention to produce complete or grammatical sentences. We break off, we forget how we began, we confuse two or more constructions, etc. Nevertheless, the interpretation of all of these depends upon their relation to the sentences of the grammar. We can only recognise sentence fragments, or incomplete or ungrammatical sentences, if we know what a complete grammatical sentence is.

In spite of the remarks at the beginning of this section, it is useful to think of both words and sentences as having meaning. Moreover, the meaning of a sentence can be predicted from the meaning of the words it contains, or, more strictly, from these words qua lexemes and the grammatical features with which they are associated. (But there has been some debate whether the meaning is to be related to the actual SURFACE STRUCTURE or some more abstract DEEP STRUCTURE – see 6.1.) So each sentence will have a meaning (a 'literal' meaning), or, if it is ambiguous like *I went to the bank*, two or more meanings. However, there are other kinds of meaning that are not directly related to grammatical and lexical structure. There is more to the problem of meaning than saying that *The cat sat on the mat* means 'The cat sat on the mat'.

First, a great deal of meaning in the spoken language is carried by the PROSODIC and PARALINGUISTIC features of language – intonation, stress, rhythm, loudness, etc., as well as such features as facial expressions and gestures (which are often called 'paralinguistic' in a wide sense of the term). We can, for instance, by the appropriate use of intonation, be sarcastic, so that *That's very clever* means 'That's not very clever'. We can also imply what is not said. Thus *I don't like coffee* with a fall-rise intonation may well imply 'I like tea' and *She's very clever* may suggest 'She's rather ugly'. Or we can indicate that what we are saying is not really true, but is just meant to tease, by winking or even by simply smiling.

Secondly, we can by various devices, including intonation, indicate what is important, contrastive or new. The difference between *I sáw John this morning*, *I saw Jóhn this morning* and *I saw John this mórning* does not concern the information itself, but the relation between that information and previous information known to speaker and hearer. The choice of an active or passive sentence, *The car hit the child* or *The child was hit by the car*, may relate to what it is that we are talking about, and we can draw attention to items by change of word order as in *That one I don't like* as opposed to *I don't like that one*.

Thirdly, there is a variety of what are today called 'speech acts'. We warn, we threaten, we promise, though often without giving any overt indication that we are doing so. The classic example is *There is a bull in the field*, which could be meant as a warning, not simply as a piece of information.

Fourthly (and this is a more general point than the one just made), we can often 'say' one thing and 'mean' another. To say of a professional athlete or a leader of industry *He is a nice man* may well be meant to suggest that he is not really very good at his profession. In general, giving irrelevant information can be taken to suggest that more relevant information would be unfavourable.

Fifthly, there is a problem associated with sentences like *Have you stopped beating your wife?* It is impossible to answer *Yes* or *No* without admitting that you have beaten her in the past. For the question implies or presupposes that you did, though it does not actually say so. Similarly, it has been argued that *The King of France is bald* presupposes that there is a King of France, though it does not assert his existence, while both *I regret that she came* and *I don't regret that she came* presuppose that she came.

Finally, language is often deeply concerned with a variety of social relations. We can be rude or polite, and the decision to be one or the other may depend upon the social relationship with the person to whom we are speaking. Thus we may ask for silence with *Shut up*, *Be quiet*, *Would you please be quiet?*, *Would you keep your voice down a little please?* The choice depends on whether we wish to be rude or not – and this relates to the status of the person addressed. Some parts of language are wholly social and carry no information (even if we include giving orders, etc., within information) at all. Examples are *Good morning*, *How are you?*, and all the Englishman's remarks about the weather. In some societies replies and questions are often about the family, but no real information is being sought – the speaker does not want to know about the health of the family of the man he is talking to, but is simply making social contact. Even a great deal of 'small talk' at parties is really of the same kind. It is not intended to transmit information, but is simply part of the social activity. As W. S. Gilbert said (*Patience*):

> The meaning doesn't matter
> If it's only idle chatter
> Of a transcendental kind.

Lyons (1977: 643) has suggested that we should draw a distinction between sentence meaning and utterance meaning, the sentence meaning being directly predictable from the grammatical and lexical features of the sentence, while utterance meaning includes all the various types of meaning that we have just been discussing. The distinction is a useful one, but there are two reservations. First, we cannot always clearly decide what is sentence meaning and what is utterance meaning. In principle it could be argued that the intonation of a sentence is part of its grammatical form, and that intonation signals sentence meaning, not utterance meaning, a sarcastic intonation having the same function as a negative. Yet in practice the prosodic and paralinguistic features are so varied and so variable in what they signal that it is advisable not to attempt to include them within the grammatical analysis. Equally it could be argued that presuppositional meaning is contained in the lexical and grammatical characteristics of the sentence: *stop* includes in its meaning that the activity was being carried on previously, while any noun phrase, such as *The King of France*, indicates that the item referred to exists (see 7.4). Secondly, the term 'utterance' is a little misleading. Utterances are usually taken to be unique speech events and no two utterances are the same. But the linguist is concerned with making generalisations about them and should not be misled by Heraclitus' dictum 'You can't step into the same river twice.' When he generalises, he talks about sentences. If then I say 'It's a fine day', although this may be a single utterance, it is interesting only as an instance of the sentence *It is a fine day*. Indeed an utterance cannot even be recognised (though it can be stored on a tape) without being presented in sentence form. What Lyons means by utterance meaning, then, is the part of the meaning of a sentence that is not directly related to the grammatical and lexical features, but is obtained either from associated prosodic and paralinguistic features or from the context, linguistic and non-linguistic, in which it occurs. But he is still generalising. He is not concerned with a particular utterance 'There is a bull in the field' which was uttered as a warning at a particular time by a particular person, but with *There is a bull in the field*, or at least with the CLASS of utterances that can be identified in terms of the sentence *There is a bull in the field* and are used as a warning. With these reservations the distinction IS a useful one, and I shall use 'Utterance meaning' as the title of Chapter 7, where all the types of meaning that we have been considering will be discussed in detail.

For some scholars it is not the sentence but the PROPOSITION that is the basic unit of semantics. One reason for this is the belief that semantics must be TRUTH-CONDITIONAL, and that propositions, unlike sentences, can always be characterised as true or false (see 8.5). One argument in favour of the distinction is that a sentence such as *I was there yesterday* may be uttered at different times and different places by different people, and may, for instance, assert that Bill Smith was in London on 18 January 1980 or that Mary Brown was in Bristol on 18 August 1981. This sentence cannot, therefore, be said to be true or false, but the various propositions that it states (concerning Bill Smith and Mary Brown) can be. Logic, moreover, which is truth-conditional, is not concerned with the grammatical and lexical forms of the sentence, but essentially with its propositional meaning. Thus *Every boy loves some girl* is grammatically unambiguous, but for the logician it expresses two quite distinct propositions – either that every boy loves a different girl or that every boy loves the same girl. This is important because different logical inferences can be drawn from these distinct propositions.

It has also been pointed out that we seem to distinguish between sentences and propositions in the distinction between direct and indirect speech. Thus, while *John said 'I'll come on Tuesday'* is true only if 'I'll come on Tuesday' were his actual words, *John said he would come on Tuesday* is true if the information is correct. John may have said 'I'll be there on Tuesday' or he may have spoken in French. The verb *say* is thus ambiguous: it may refer either to the actual words that were spoken (which will be shown in quotation marks) or to the propositional content of the words uttered (usually introduced by *that*).

There are, however, grave difficulties in restricting semantics to propositions. To begin with, all the kinds of utterance meaning that we have discussed will be outside semantics. More seriously, we shall be restricted to statements, while questions and commands are excluded even though, in actual language, questions and commands are just as important as statements. Language is not simply concerned with providing information. We should have nothing to say, moreover, concerning MODALITY (6.8) – the judgments we make about possible states of affairs as in *John may be in his office*, which indicates the speaker's attitude towards the probability of John being in his office. Even the argument concerning *I was there yesterday* can be turned on its head and used against the notion of proposition, for there are very serious doubts whether sentences containing words such as *I*, *there* and *yesterday* (these are called DEICTICS – see 3.5), which take their meaning from the context, can ever be accurately stated in propositional terms. If that is so, semantics restricted to propositions will be extraordinarily limited, for ordinary language is full of such deictic terms.

Finally, it is obvious that when we wish to refer to propositions we normally do so in terms of sentences – as is clear from all our examples. Even if logical formulae are used, they are no more than translations of sentences into a logical 'language'. This should make us wonder whether propositions are either necessary or justified. The only real advantage they offer is that they may avoid some ambiguities, but that can be done no less easily by talking about 'sentences with a particular interpretation', by recognising, that is to say, and indicating precisely, those ambiguities that may be troublesome.

3

CONTEXT AND REFERENCE

In the last chapter a distinction was drawn between reference, which deals with the relations between language and the non-linguistic world of experience, and sense, which deals with relations within language. Linguists and philosophers have, on the whole, been more concerned with sense relations. These appear, superficially at least, to be easier to handle than reference; a great deal of this book will, in consequence, be concerned with sense. Yet most people would think that meaning was primarily (or even wholly) concerned with the relation between language and the world in which we use it, and this is the topic of this chapter. I shall, however, be using the term 'reference' in the restricted sense suggested in 2.1, and shall talk about the relation of language to the world in terms of CONTEXT, or, to distinguish it from linguistic context, CONTEXT OF SITUATION.

3.1 *Linguistic relativity*

Part of the difficulty in relating language to the external world may arise from the fact that the way in which we see the world is to some degree dependent on the language we use. Since we categorise the objects of our experience with the aid of language, it may be the case that learning about the world and learning about language are activities that cannot be separated and that therefore our world is partly determined by our language. Indeed Malinowski (see 3.3) argued that primitive people have names only for those things that stand out for them from an otherwise 'undifferentiated world'. From a confused mass of experience, so to speak, they pick out by words those parts that are relevant to them.

Some scholars have taken a fairly extreme position on this. Sapir (1929 [1949: 160]), for instance, suggested that the world in which we live 'is to a large extent unconsciously built up on the language habits of the group'. His view was expanded and explained by Whorf and became known as the 'Sapir–Whorf hypothesis'. Whorf argued that we are unaware of the background character of our language, just as we are unaware of the presence of air until we begin to choke, and that if we look at other languages we come to realise that a language does not merely voice ideas, but that it is 'the shaper of ideas' and that we 'dissect nature along lines laid down by our native languages'. This led him to a 'new principle of relativity which holds that all observers are not led by the same physical evidence to the same picture of the universe, unless their linguistic backgrounds are similar or in some way can be calibrated' (1956: 214).

In the same article, 'Science and linguistics' (1956: 207–19), Whorf produces evidence of several kinds for his view. First, he suggests that there is no division in reality corresponding to English nouns and verbs. For why do we use nouns for *lightning, spark, wave, eddy, pulsation, flame, storm, phase, cycle, spasm, noise, emotion?* In the American Indian language Hopi all events of brief duration (mostly included in the English nouns above) are represented by verbs. In another American Indian language there is no noun/verb distinction at all; instead of 'There is a house' the form is (in translation) 'A house occurs' or better 'It houses'. Secondly, as we have already noted (2.1), Hopi has one word for insect, pilot and plane while Eskimo has four words for snow. We could add that some forms of Arabic have a large number of words (reputedly a hundred) for 'camel'. Thirdly, Whorf argued, their language shows that the Hopi have no notion of time. The only distinction they make is between what is subjective and what objective, the subjective including both the future and everything that is 'mental'. No distinction, moreover, is made (in the language and, therefore, by the Hopi themselves) between distance in time and distance in place.

It is not clear whether Sapir and Whorf thought that the 'shape' of the world was totally determined by our language, i.e. that without language it has no shape at all. Such an extreme interpretation is untenable for the same kind of reason as is the nominalist view of words as mere names of things. For if language classifies and categorises experience it must do so on the basis of some language-independent characteristic of that experience. In some sense, then, there is a world that we must share irrespective of the language we use. Moreover, unless there is some recognisable non-linguistic world of experience it is difficult to see how we could either learn a language or use it with our neighbours consistently.

Whorf's arguments as they stand are not wholly convincing. If we do not have the 'same picture of the universe' as the speakers of other languages, we nevertheless have a picture that can be related to and in some degree 'mapped upon' the picture that others have. That this is so is proved by the fact that we can investigate other languages (as Whorf did!), and that we can translate. It may well be that we can never totally absorb or understand the 'world' of other languages, but it is clear enough that we can obtain a very fair understanding of them. This we could not do if the pictures were totally different. Similarly, we often meet difficulties in translation, but we never totally fail to translate from one language to another. There may be no exact equivalence, but languages are never totally different.

Much of Whorf's argument, moreover, is invalid in that he argues from certain formal observable grammatical characteristics to a 'model of the Universe'. His Hopi model is very largely based upon the verbal system. But by a similar argument we could argue that English too has no concept of time. If we define tense in terms of forms of verbs, English has two tenses only, present and past (see Palmer 1974: 36–7). All other so-called tenses involve the use of auxiliary verbs – *was loving, will love, has loved*, etc. Nor does past tense, defined in this way, relate only to past time as in *I went there yesterday*, for it is also used for 'unreality' as in *If I went tomorrow, I should see him* or *I wish I went there every day*. It has been actually suggested (Joos 1964: 121) that English does not have a past tense, but a 'remote' tense to indicate what is remote in time or remote in reality. This would make English more like Hopi, and it is easy to see that, if English had been an American Indian language, it could have been used as an example of a language in which time relations are not distinguished. But few of us would believe that English speakers fail to make such time distinctions. It is clear that the grammatical structure of a language tells us little about our way of thinking about the world.

In spite of these objections the Sapir–Whorf hypothesis serves a useful purpose in reminding us that the categories we employ do not simply 'exist' in the world of experience. Although it may not be true that language actually determines our world, at least we cannot distinguish clearly between what is 'in' the world and what is 'in' language. The sense relations that were discussed in 2.3 should not be regarded as mere reflections of reality; for such a view would again involve us in all the problems encountered with a naming theory of meaning. Although difference of sex may be thought of as a purely physical difference that is simply mirrored in *bull/cow*, *stallion/mare*, *ewe/ram*, age distinctions are far less objectively 'real', and alongside *calf*, *foal*, *lamb*, we find *heifer*, *steer*, *colt*, *filly*, *teg* ('two-year-old sheep'), etc., as well as the adult names. Such distinctions can hardly be said to exist in the world. There are some sense relations that have very little reality. It would be difficult to recognise the worldly counterparts of *come/go*, *bring/take* (3.5), and, of course, as was seen in 2.1, different languages have different sets of words and so different semantic structures. We shall return to the problem later (5.8).

3.2 *The exclusion of context*

We have already noted that there are linguists who, explicitly or implicitly, exclude context from the study of semantics. The real reason, no doubt, for this exclusion is that there are

extremely great theoretical and practical difficulties in handling context satisfactorily. But reasons other than these are
often given, and these we will now consider.

First, it is argued that the meaning of a sentence, or the
fact that it is ambiguous or anomalous, can be known in
isolation from any context, and that as speakers of a language
we must know the meaning of a sentence before we can use it
in any given context; meaning is thus shown to be independent of context and linguists can, and must, study it without
reference to context. This argument, however, begs the
question. For in what sense could it be argued that we know
the meaning of a sentence independently of the context?
Presumably, only in the sense that we can provide another
sentence of similar meaning, a paraphrase of it. But it in no
way follows that if we can identify two sentences as having
the same meaning, we have, thereby, identified some abstract entity called 'meaning'. This is another version of the
dualist fallacy that we discussed at the end of 2.2. Instead, it
might well be argued that knowing that two sentences are
similar in meaning is knowing that they can be used in similar
contexts. In that case, to set up a set of abstract relationships
between sentences without even considering what it is that
they refer to, is rather like describing all the equivalences in a
measuring system, e.g. that there are 12 inches in a foot,
3 feet in a yard, 1760 yards in a mile, without even indicating
how long an inch, a foot, a yard or a mile actually is. Stating
meaning equivalence is not stating meaning, and there is no
proof that knowing the meaning of a sentence does not entail
knowing the context in which it is used.

A second and, at first sight, rather more plausible
argument is that the world of experience must of necessity
include the sum of human knowledge. If this is so, and if
semantics is defined in terms of context, the scope of semantics will be infinite. This is a problem of which Bloomfield
was aware, and it made him despair of any satisfactory treatment of semantics. But the problem is one that is raised for
any kind of comprehensive theory of semantics. It is no less

acute for a theory based on sense relations than one based on reference, for it is impossible even in that theory to draw a clear line between the meaning of a word or sentence and all the possibly relevant information about it. We can evade the problem by confining our attention to 'tight' lexical relationships of the kind seen in *unmarried/bachelor* or *short/long*, but this will provide a very narrow semantic theory that can hardly be said to deal properly with meaning. For consider the sense relations involved in Bierwisch's *My typewriter has bad intentions* (which is anomalous) and *John was looking for the glasses* (which is ambiguous). To recognise the anomaly and the ambiguity we need to have the relevant information about typewriters and kinds of glasses.

To make this point clear let us consider, in a little detail, part of the argument of Katz & Fodor (1963: 174–9). It will be remembered that part of the aim of semantics according to them was to 'account for the number of readings of a sentence'. An example they used was *The bill is large*. This is clearly ambiguous – it has two 'readings' resulting from the two meanings of *bill*. The sentence can, however, be 'disambiguated', i.e. one or other of its two readings can be established, if we extend it with . . . *but need not be paid*. This extension is, of course, possible only with one of the meanings of *bill*. Now Katz & Fodor accept that the ambiguity of this sentence and its disambiguation by this method are proper subjects for semantics. Yet the discussion of them is immediately followed by the argument against a 'complete theory of settings' (i.e. context), that such a theory would have to represent all the knowledge that speakers have about the world. For, the argument goes, ANY kind of non-linguistic information may be used in the understanding of a sentence. One set of examples they use to show this is *Shall we take junior back to the zoo?*, *Shall we take the bus back to the zoo?*, *Shall we take the lion back to the zoo?* To understand these, it is suggested, we have to know all about boys, buses and lions, and such information cannot properly be included in a semantic theory. Yet a moment's reflection will show that

the position is no different than with *bill*. For here we need
the information that there are two kinds of bill, while, conversely, we can show the meaning differences of the other
sentences by extending them with . . . *to see the other animals?, . . . or walk?, . . . or put it in our own cage?* We can
always invent extensions to sentences to deal with any kind of
'meaning' relating to any kind of information that may be
relevant. If this is so, and if the use of such extensions is a
valid method of establishing sense relations, it follows that
ANY kind of information can be the basis of a sense relation
and that sense, no less than reference, ultimately involves the
whole of human knowledge.

Let us again consider Bierwisch's *John was looking for the
glasses*. This is ambiguous because it might refer to spectacles
or to drinking glasses. But why should there be just two
meanings? What if a scientist has yet a third type? Does the
sentence now have three meanings? If it does, it does so
because of our knowledge of the world. Similarly, how many
meanings has *I am looking for the bible*? The answer depends
on whether you know that one of the cow's stomachs is called
the bible! Similarly, let us take Bierwisch's anomalous example *My typewriter has bad intentions*, and replace *typewriter*
by *dog*, *snake* and *microbe*. Whether the resulting sentence is
judged to be anomalous can be determined only by what we
know about the intelligence of dogs, snakes and microbes.
The anomaly depends, that is to say, on knowledge of the
world.

It is, of course, perfectly reasonable to take a methodological decision to restrict one's attention, for a time, to sense
relations, as we shall be doing in Chapter 5. It is also a purely
terminological question whether the term *semantics* is to be
used only for the study of sense relations (or truth conditions). But we ought not to make a theoretical decision to
treat such a restricted form of semantics as more central to
the study of language. For first, if we use only the highly
structured aspects of sense relations, only a small part of
meaning will ever be captured, since much of what is found

in dictionaries does not fall neatly into patterns of the kind that have been illustrated (and if we think of all dictionary definitions as sense relations we shall find that sense is as limitless as reference in terms of the totality of human knowledge). Secondly, as we have seen, it is not possible to draw a clear theoretical division between what is in the world and what is in the language. If, moreover, we think that we are concerned with the speaker's knowledge (as Katz & Fodor do) it is, surely, almost certain that the speaker does not separate, in his use of language, his knowledge of semantic structure and his knowledge of the world.

3.3 *Context of situation*

The term *context of situation* is associated with two scholars, first an anthropologist who has already been mentioned, Malinowski, and later a linguist, Firth. Both were concerned with stating meaning in terms of the context in which language is used, but in rather different ways.

Malinowski's interest in language derived from his work in the Trobriand Islands in the South Pacific. He was particularly concerned with his failure to produce any satisfactory translations for the texts he had recorded. For instance, he recorded a boast by a canoeist which he translated, 'We-run front-wood ourselves . . . we-turn we-see companion-ours he-runs rear-wood.' This, Malinowski argued (1923 [1949: 300–1]), made sense only if the utterance was seen in the context in which it was used, where it would become clear that, for instance, 'wood' referred to the paddle of the canoe. Living languages must not be treated like dead ones, torn from their context of situation, but seen as used by people for hunting, cultivating, looking for fish, etc. Language as used in books is not at all the norm; it represents a far-fetched derivative function of language, for language was not originally a 'mirror of reflected thought'. Language is, he maintained, a 'mode of action' not a 'countersign of thought'.

Malinowski's arguments were primarily based on his

observation of the way in which the language of the people he was studying fitted into their everyday activities, and was thus an inseparable part of them. But he noted also that there is, even in our own more sophisticated society, a special significance of expressions such as *How do you do?*, *Ah, here you are*, which are used to establish a common sentiment. We saw some examples of this – talk about the weather or the family – in 2.5. This aspect of language he called 'phatic communion', where the words do not convey meaning but have a purely social function.

He noted, too, that the child, right from the stage of babbling, uses words as 'active forces' with which to manipulate the world around him. For the primitive man, similarly, words are 'important utensils'. Indeed for him, Malinowski argued, there is much in common between words and magic, for both give him power.

Malinowski's remarks about language as a mode of action are useful in reminding us that language is not simply a matter of stating information. But there are two reasons why we cannot wholly accept his arguments. First, he believed that the 'mode of action' aspect of language was most clearly seen in the 'basic' needs of man as illustrated in the languages of the child or of primitive man. He assumed that the language he was considering was more primitive than our own and thus more closely associated with the practical needs of the primitive society. To a very large degree, therefore, he assumed that the difficulties of translation were due to the differences in the nature of the languages and that the need to invoke context of situation was more important when dealing with primitive languages. But he was mistaken. For although there may be 'primitive' people, who lack the knowledge and skill of civilised people, there is no sense in which a language can be regarded as primitive. Of course many languages may not have the vocabulary of modern industrial society, but this is a reflection of the interests of the society, not of the primitive nature of the language. In purely linguistic terms it appears to be a fact that no one language can be judged more primitive than another – though Malinowski is by no means the only scholar to make this false assumption. The difficulties of translation that Malinowski noted result only from the DIFFERENCES between the languages, not the fact that one is more primitive. Secondly, Malinowski's views do not provide the basis of any workable semantic theory. He does not even discuss the ways in which context can be handled in a systematic way, to provide a statement of meaning. Moreover, it is quite clear that even with his Trobriand Islanders much of their linguistic activity is not easily related to context. For instance, he discusses narrative, the telling of stories; but here, surely, the context is the same at all times – the story teller and his audience, whatever the story. If context is to be taken as an indication of meaning, all stories will have the same meaning. Malinowski's solution was to invoke 'secondary context', the context within the narrative; but that has no immediately observable status and can no more be objectively defined than the concepts or thoughts that he was so eager to banish from discussion.

Firth acknowledged his debt to Malinowski, but felt that Malinowski's context of situation was not satisfactory for the more accurate and precise linguistic approach to the problem. For Malinowski's context of situation was 'a bit of the social process which can be considered apart' or 'an ordered series of events *in rebus*' (i.e. an ACTUAL observable set of events). Firth preferred to see context of situation as part of the linguist's apparatus in the same way as are the grammatical categories that he uses. It was best used as 'a suitable schematic construct' to apply to language events and he, therefore, suggested the following categories (Firth 1950: 43–4 [1957a: 182]; 1957b: 9 [1968: 177]):

A. The relevant features of the participants: persons, personalities
   (i) The verbal action of the participants.
   (ii) The non-verbal action of the participants.

B.   The relevant objects.

C.   The effects of the verbal action.

In this way contexts of situation can be grouped and classified; this is essential if it is to be part of the linguistic analysis of a language.

As an example of his use of context of situation Firth considered a 'typical' Cockney event with the sentence:

Ahng gunna gi' wun fer Ber'.

'I'm going to get one for Bert.'

'What', he asks, 'is the minimum number of participants? Three? Four? Where might it happen? In a pub? Where is Bert? Outside? Or playing darts? What are the relevant objects? What is the effect of the sentence? "Obvious!" you say.'

It is important to stress that Firth saw context of situation as one part of the linguist's apparatus or rather as one of the techniques of description, grammar being another such technique on a different level, but of the same abstract nature. For linguistics was for him a sort of hierarchy of such techniques all of which made statements of meaning. Here he used the analogy of the spectrum in which light is dispersed into its various wavelengths; linguistics similarly would 'disperse' meaning in a 'spectrum of specialized statements'. Thus, for Firth all kinds of linguistic description, the phonology, the grammar, etc., as well as the context of situation, were statements of meaning. Describing meaning in terms of context of situation is, then, just one of the ways in which a linguist handles a language, and not in principle very different from the other ways in which he carries out his task.

It has often been said that Firth was guilty of equivocation in his use of the word 'meaning'. For while context of situation may well deal with meaning in the usual sense, i.e. the 'semantic' sense, quite clearly the other levels, grammar, etc., are not concerned with meaning in the same sense. In claiming, therefore, that all the levels are statements of meaning and that context of situation was thus just one of a set of similar levels, Firth was, consciously or unconsciously, using 'meaning' in two different senses, one legitimate, the other his own idiosyncratic usage.

This criticism is not entirely fair. For, first, we have already seen in the discussion of sense and reference (2.3) that it is almost certainly impossible, in principle, to decide what is 'in the world' and what is 'in language'. If this is so, Firth is surely to be praised rather than criticised for refusing to draw a clear distinction within his levels of description between the one that deals with language and the world and those that are wholly within language. Secondly, Firth did not produce any total, 'monolithic', linguistic model which could, in theory at least, totally describe a language. He did not believe that such a model was possible even in principle (though nearly all linguists have assumed that such a model is not merely possible, but essential). Firth believed that the linguist merely makes partial statements of meaning, saying what he can about language where he can, cutting into it at different places like cutting a cake. If this is so, there is no need to distinguish between statements that are about meaning and those that are not.

A more serious criticism of Firth's view is that it has very limited value. Context of situation may be all right for the Cockney example or for the drill sergeant's *Stand at – ease*, but not for the vast majority of the sentences that we encounter. But this does not prove that Firth was wrong. If we cannot get very far with context of situation this is perhaps no more than a reflection of the difficulty of saying anything about semantics, and it is surely better to say a little than to say nothing at all. It must be remembered too that Firth believed we could never capture the whole of meaning. One virtue of Firth's approach was that he set out to make only PARTIAL statements of meaning. It may be that this is all we can ever hope to achieve. It is easy enough to be scornful, as some scholars have been, of contextual theories and to dismiss them as totally unworkable. But it is difficult to see how we can dismiss them without denying the obvious fact that the meaning of words and sentences relate to the world of our experience.

3.4 *Behaviourism*

Malinowski and Firth believed that the description of a language could not be complete without some reference to the context of situation in which the language operated. A more extreme view sees the meaning of the linguistic elements as TOTALLY accounted for in terms of the situation in which it is used.

This is BEHAVIOURISM, associated first in linguistics with Bloomfield. Bloomfield's starting point was not so much his observation of language events as his belief in the 'scientific' nature of his subject and he maintained that the only useful generalisations about language are 'inductive' generalisations (1933: 20). He defined the meaning of a linguistic form as 'the situation in which the speaker utters it and the response it calls forth in the hearer'. This is going much further than either Malinowski or Firth. They made statements of meaning in terms of the situation. Bloomfield is, essentially, defining meaning AS the situation.

Bloomfield (1933: 22–7) illustrated his views with a now famous account of Jack and Jill. Jill is hungry, sees an apple and with the use of language gets Jack to fetch it for her. If she had been alone (or if she had not been human) she would have first received a STIMULUS (S) which would have produced a REACTION (R) (the term RESPONSE is more usual) – she would have made a move to get the apple. This can be diagrammed:

Since, however, Jack was with her, the stimulus produced not the reaction R, but a linguistic reaction, that of speaking to Jack, which we may symbolise by r. The sound waves resulting from this in turn created a stimulus for Jack, a linguistic stimulus (s), which results in his non-linguistic

reaction R of getting the apple. We now have a more complicated picture.

S ⟶ r . . . . s ⟶ R

Meaning, according to Bloomfield, consists in the relation
between speech (which is shown by r . . . s) and the practical
events (S) and (R) that precede and follow it.

One important point for the theory is that the stimulus and
the reaction are physical events. For Jill it is a matter of light
waves striking her eyes, of her muscles contracting and of
fluids being secreted in her stomach. Jack's action is no less
physical. For part of Bloomfield's thesis is that human behaviour, including speech, is controlled by the same physical,
wholly deterministic, laws as other events in the universe.
Bloomfield was at great pains to contrast his 'mechanistic'
theory with the 'mentalistic' theories that posit non-physical
processes such as thoughts, concepts, images, feelings, etc.
He did not deny that we have such images, feelings, etc., but
explained them as popular terms for bodily movements,
events that the speaker alone is aware of (as in *I'm hungry*),
private experiences (obscure internal stimuli), or soundless
movements of the vocal organs. Of course Jill might not have
acted in the same way if she had been bashful, and Jack might
not have fetched the apple if he had been ill-disposed towards
her. It was necessary, therefore, for the situation to include
all the relevant features of the relation between Jack and Jill.
Bloomfield accounted for this by arguing that the speech and
the practical events depend upon 'predisposing factors'
which consist of 'the entire life history of the speaker and
hearer'. These predisposing factors must, however, carry a
great deal of the weight of explaining the linguistic facts. For
not only may the same apparent situation produce quite
different linguistic responses but also the same linguistic
response may occur in quite different situations. Bloomfield
himself (1926: 153) had noted that *I'm hungry* might be
uttered not only by someone who really was hungry but also
by a naughty child who did not want to go to bed.

Now it may well be that ultimately all activity is, in principle, explainable in terms of physical entities and events, the
chemistry, electro-magnetism, etc., involved in the cells of
the human brain. It seems probable that our experiences are
recorded in some way by changes in the state of the brain.
But this is, in the light of present human knowledge, no more
than an act of faith, a simple belief in the physical nature of all
human activity. For linguistics, however, the theory has no
value. The facts, especially those concerning predisposing
factors, are totally unknowable and no more open to observation than the thoughts, images, etc., of the mentalists that
Bloomfield despised. In the present state of our knowledge
talking about predisposing factors involves the same circularity of argument as talking about concepts (2.2).

Bloomfield had a curious and rather misplaced faith in
science and scientific description. He forecast (quite incorrectly as it turned out) that all the problems of phonology
would be solved in a few decades in the phonetics laboratory.
More pertinently, he suggested that we can define the meaning of a speech form accurately 'when this meaning has to do
with some matter of which we possess scientific knowledge'
and gave as an example the 'ordinary meaning of salt' as
'sodium chloride (NaCl)' (see 2.1). Apart from the fact that it
is not clear how this meaning is related to the model of
meaning illustrated by Jack and Jill (possibly a matter of
ostensive definition?), it is clear that Bloomfield was wrong.
There is no reason at all to argue that scientific definitions are
LINGUISTICALLY more accurate than non-scientific ones. The
precision of scientific definition serves the scientist's purpose, but it is in no way related to human language; it is no
part of linguistics to tidy up language by making it more
'scientific' in this way.

Bloomfield's theory loses its force when we realise how
many of the relevant predisposing factors are unknown and
unknowable. A much more elaborate theory, which claims to
overcome this difficulty, is that of Skinner (1957). The essential arguments (though it is impossible to do them justice in a

brief summary) are (1) that language behaviour can be accounted for in a way that is in principle no different from the behaviour of rats in laboratory conditions, and (2) that the behaviour can be explained in terms of observable events, without reference to the internal structure of the organism. The basic notions are stimulus, response and REINFORCE-MENT. The laboratory rat presses a lever and receives a pellet of food. The fact that the rat will come to do this regularly is explained by saying that the receipt of the pellet is a particular kind of stimulus – a REINFORCING EVENT, which increases the strength of the response. The whole of learning, including language learning and all subsequent behaviour, can be explained in the same way. Instead of Bloomfield's predisposing factors we need a history of reinforcing events to account for the way we behave.

Unfortunately, this theory runs into difficulties of a similar kind. For while it is easy enough to identify the stimuli, the responses and the reinforcing events in the laboratory, much of human behaviour (as well as the natural behaviour of other creatures), and especially language, is enormously more complex, and it is largely impossible to identify the relevant events. We are once again in danger of simply postulating hypothetical concepts that would 'explain' what we can observe. There is a well-known and amusing passage in a review by Chomsky (1959) of Skinner's proposals. He discusses the possibility that on seeing a picture someone may say 'Dutch'. We thus have the stimulus (the picture), and the (linguistic) response. But Chomsky points out that in fact a whole variety of responses are possible including 'Clashes with the wallpaper', or 'Remember our camping trip last summer'. The variety of responses can only be explained if it is argued that the controlling stimuli are also different, including, of course, all the history of reinforcing events. But there is no way, even in principle, that we can identify these except by working backwards from the observable responses and establishing as stimuli whatever would be needed to produce the required responses. But the responses are then no longer predictable from the stimuli and the theory becomes vacuous. Without prediction there is no scientific explanation.

It is, of course, true that some aspects of early learning, even of language, can be explained in behaviourist terms. The child learns that making certain noises will have desired results such as food and attention from his parents. His utterances can thus be seen as reinforced responses. But the child very rapidly leaves the stage where a simple behaviourist account of his language can be given, and we have little understanding of the way in which this comes about.

3.5 *Context, culture and style*

Instead of trying to interpret meaning in terms of context, we can set ourselves the much more limited task of identifying those features of context which seem to be most relevant to our choice of language.

To begin with, most, and perhaps all, languages have deictics (see 2.5), which identify objects, persons and events in terms of their relation to the speaker in space and time. There are three main types of deictic.

First, the speaker must be able to identify the participants in the discourse – himself and the person or persons to whom he is speaking. The forms with which he achieves this are the first and second person pronouns – *I/we* and *you* respectively in English. The choice of pronoun is, however, often involved with other, social, factors and we will, therefore, leave detailed discussion until a little later.

Secondly, English has *here* and *there*, *this* and *that* to distinguish between the position of the speaker or closeness to it and other positions or greater distances. The exact spatial relationship indicated by such words will vary according to the language. In Malagasy, for instance, the choice of the words *ety* and *aty* which may be translated 'here' and 'there' (*Ety ny tranony* 'His house is here', *Aty ny tranony* 'His house is there') depends on whether the object in question is visible or not to the speaker (Keenan 1971: 45). Spatial relations, moreover, may often determine more than simply such words as *here/there*, *this/that*. English has the pair of verbs *come* and *go* (Fillmore 1966). *Come* is restricted in a way that *go* is not, in that it indicates direction towards the speaker or hearer. It is used, first, for simple direction towards speaker or hearer as in *Come to me* and *I'll come to you*. But, secondly, it is also used for direction towards speaker or hearer at the time of the relevant event, either in the past or the future (as well as the present) – *He came to me in London*, *I'll come to see you in Paris (when you get there)*. Thirdly, it is used to refer to direction to a place at which the speaker or hearer is habitually found, even if he is not there at the relevant time, e.g. *Come to my office (though I shan't be there)*, *I came to your house (but you were out)*. In this third case *go* is also possible, *Go to my office*, *I went to your house*. Moreover, if the reference is to motion AWAY from the position of the relevant person, *go* would be much more normal. I could hardly say *Come to my office immediately*, if the person I am addressing is with me in some place other than my office, since the motion is then clearly away from me. Similarly we should not normally say *He left you at his house and came to yours*, for again the motion is away from the relevant person. If there is no indication at all of the position of either hearer or speaker, *go* will be used. *Come* and *go* are not the only pair of verbs with these characteristics. *Bring* and *take* function in exactly the same way, with the additional meaning of 'carry'.

Thirdly, time relations are indicated in English not only by general adverbs such as *now* and *then* but also by more specific ones such as *yesterday* and *tomorrow*. Moreover, such time relations are often incorporated into the grammar of the verb – as is the case with most European languages. But although some languages have a clear threefold distinction of present, past and future, e.g. Latin *amo*, *amabo*, *amabam* or *amavi*, it is worth noting that in English the present/past distinction is more central than the distinction between these and the future. For it is only the present/past distinction that is made by inflection of the verb (*love/loved*); the future has to be indicated by the use of periphrastic forms such as *will love* or *is going to love*. Even the adverbs *now* and *then* have no single-word counterpart to refer to the future. Moreover, as we shall see in 6.3, tense is often closely associated in languages with aspect (which is not deictic) and mood (which is highly subjective).

Deictics cannot be ignored in the study of meaning, for ordinary language is full of their use. But, as we noted, in 2.5, they raise problems for any kind of analysis that treats propositions or statements (categorical assertions) as somehow basic to semantics. For deictics are always subjective in the sense that they can be interpreted only with reference to the speaker, while propositions are, by their definition, wholly objective and independent of speakers.

Another very important aspect of context is that provided by social relations. It is often not enough for the speaker to be able to identify the person to whom he is speaking; he must, in many languages, also indicate quite clearly the social relations between himself and this person. In many European languages particularly (but not exclusively), we can distinguish between a polite and a familiar second person pronoun for addressing a single person. The polite form is either what is grammatically or historically the second person plural form or a third person form. Thus French, Greek and Russian use the plural forms, *tu/vous*, *esi/esis*, *ty/vy* (while English has lost the singular form *thou* altogether). Italian and Spanish use third person forms and thus still retain the singular/plural distinction – *tu/Lei* and *voi/Loro*, *tu/ustéd* and *vos/ustédes*. If the pronouns are not expressed, the distinction between second and third person is lost, as has been noted for colloquial Brazilian Portuguese as in *janta* 'you/he/she lunch(es)', *jantam* 'you/they lunch' (Hall 1964: 136).

The choice between the familiar and the polite forms, or what, following the French forms, are called the T and V forms seems to be determined by two factors, which have been termed POWER and SOLIDARITY (Brown & Gilman 1960). Power involves the asymmetric relations (see 5.1) 'older than', 'parent of', 'employer of', 'richer than', 'stronger than' and 'nobler than', while solidarity involves such symmetric relations as 'attended the same school', 'have the same parents', 'practise the same profession'. Where there is power, the more powerful uses T to address the less powerful, while the less powerful uses V in his reply; where there is solidarity the T form is used. There may, of course, be conflict: an elder brother will be in a position of both power and solidarity in relation to a younger one, or there may be hierarchical relations within a profession. It seems fairly clear, however, that, as society has become more egalitarian, power plays far less part in the determination of pronoun use, and the non-reciprocal T/V use is no longer to be found in French, German and Italian for father and son or customer and waiter relationships; instead solidarity would dictate the T forms in the first case, and lack of it would require the V forms in the second.

The conflict between solidarity and power is seen in other areas of language used for personal address. Thus, a generation or more ago it was normal for academics in Britain to use surnames for addressing one another, especially in correspondence. This was essentially a solidarity device (though a non-professorial member of staff would probably have addressed a professor with his title – a matter of power). This custom has now almost wholly disappeared except among older academics; the reason is very probably that the use of surname alone was an employer–employee power device which was felt to be objectionable by the increasing numbers of people with working-class origins who entered the profession. The solidarity device today is the use of first names, though this too has some power function, as between teacher (or parent) and child.

In some other languages much more complex linguistic systems are involved. Japanese, for instance, has its honorifics. In Korean status has to be indicated by suffixes on the verb – intimate *-na*, familiar *-e*, plain *-ta*, polite *-e yo*, deferential *-supnita*, authoritative *-so* (Trudgill 1974: 109). This status marking is a matter of the grammar of the language and is as obligatory as the marking of tense in English.

There are other characteristics of the context that affect the choice of language. (We have already noted some of these in 2.5.) Apart from the style of the individual (which they call SINGULARITY), Crystal & Davy (1969: 71–6) have suggested three main features of style – PROVINCE, STATUS and MODALITY. Province is concerned with occupation and professional activity – the language of law, science, advertising, etc. Status deals (again) with social relations, but especially in terms of the formality of language and the use of polite or colloquial language or of slang. Joos (1962) suggested there were five degrees of formality – 'frozen', 'formal', 'consultative', 'casual' and 'intimate'. Modality (though GENRE is a better term in view of the more normal use of the term *modality* in 6.8) is intended to relate to the choice between poetry and prose, essay and short story, the language of memoranda, telegrams, jokes, etc.

A competent speaker of a language must have command of all these different styles. But he will almost certainly have some command also of different kinds of his language that are collectively known as dialects. The term DIALECT has until recently been used only to refer to different forms of the language used in different geographical areas, but it has been realised that there are similar differences between the language of social classes within the same geographical area and that it is not at all easy to draw a clear distinction between these two phenomena. Sociolinguistics and dialectology are closely inter-related disciplines. Most speakers have some command of several dialects or socially distinct versions of their language. They can, moreover, switch from one to the other in the course of a conversation. A number of languages, e.g. especially Arabic, Modern Greek, Haitian Creole, and Swiss German have the phenomenon of DIGLOSSIA (Ferguson 1959), in which there are two quite distinct dialects of the language whose choice depends upon what can only be described generally as the formality of the situation. But again speakers will switch from one to the other; the interviewer on Greek television will begin by speaking Katharevousa, the formal language, but soon slips into the less formal Dhimotiki (Trudgill 1974: 118). The extreme case is that of a bilingual society where two distinct languages are in use. Within a single conversation the speakers may switch from one to the other – from English to Spanish in the case of a Puerto-Rican executive and his secretary (Fishman 1970: 37–41), or from English to Welsh, German to Frisian, etc. This practice of changing from one dialect or language to another is called CODE-SWITCHING.

The fact that a single speaker makes use of so many varieties of language raises a serious theoretical problem. It is possible to treat each variety as a different language – and this is, of course, most plausible when the differences are as great as those between the English and Spanish of the Puerto-Rican. It is least plausible where the differences are essentially those of style, for we cannot easily determine exactly how many 'languages' there are or what are their precise characteristics. In the case of diglossia even, although it may seem easy enough to determine that there are two varieties of the language, the distinction between the two is not always completely clear and speakers often seem to use language that is, in varying degrees, somewhere between the two. If, then, we decide that instead of recognising a host of different 'languages', we think rather of what is the linguistic ability of a native speaker, we must relate his choice of linguistic variety to his recognition of the relevance of context. If so, issues of code-switching, diglossia, dialect, sociolinguistics and stylistics all fall into the (widely defined) area of semantics.

In practice linguists often attempt to rule out context as far as possible – to deal with 'maximally decontextualised sentences' (Lyons 1977: 590). These are the objects of study of most grammars. On methodological grounds this is essential because of the enormous variation in language, but the dangers are obvious, and it is difficult to accept, without severe reservations, Chomsky's (1965: 3) view that 'Linguistic theory is concerned primarily with an ideal speaker–hearer, in a completely homogeneous speech community, who knows its language perfectly.'

4

LEXICAL SEMANTICS: FIELDS AND COLLOCATION

This is the first of two chapters to deal with lexical semantics. Its unifying theme is the idea that we can state the meaning of words in terms of their association with other words.

4.1 *Paradigmatic and syntagmatic*

Many of the basic ideas in this chapter derive from de Saussure's notion of VALUE. He pointed out (1916: 153[1959: 110]) that a knight on a chess board is a knight not because of any inherent quality (shape, size, etc.), but because of what it can do in relation to the other pieces on the board. He stressed this relational aspect of language, saying that there were 'only differences and no positive terms'. For instance, he argued that *sheep* in English has a different value from *mouton* in French because English has also the word *mutton*. Similarly, plural in Sanskrit has a different value from plural in French (or English), because in Sanskrit it belongs to the three-term system singular, dual, plural, while in French it belongs to a two-term system of singular and plural only. He further argued that if we consider synonyms such as *dread*, *fear*, *be afraid of*, we can say that if one of these did not exist its 'content' would go to one of the others; in other words, the field of 'fearing' is divided among three verbs (or more, of course, in actual fact), but if one were absent it would be divided between two only.

De Saussure also made the distinction between PARA-DIGMATIC and SYNTAGMATIC relations. The paradigmatic relations are those into which a linguistic unit enters through being contrasted or substitutable, in a particular environment, with other similar units. The examples we have been considering are all of a paradigmatic kind. Syntagmatic relations are those that a unit contracts by virtue of its co-occurrence with similar units. Thus, in *a red door* and *a green door*, *red* and *green* are in a paradigmatic relation to each other, while each is in a syntagmatic relation with *door*.

4.2 *Semantic fields*

In the discussion of semantic fields in this section we shall be concerned with paradigmatic relations (but see 4.4). The most famous example of field theory is that of Trier (1934) who compared the field of the 'intellectual' aspect of the German of around 1200 with that of around 1300, though there are some doubts about the accuracy of Trier's observations (see Ullmann (1962) for details). In the earlier period the field was divided into *kunst* and *list*, the former referring to courtly qualities and the second to non-courtly skills. The term *wîsheit* was used to cover the whole. In the later period, however, the field was divided into three – *wîsheit* 'religious experience', *kunst* 'knowledge' and *wizzen* 'art' (one new term, one term lost and *wîsheit* now only one part, not the whole). This is shown diagrammatically in Figure 2.

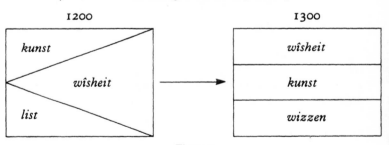

Figure 2

Trier's example compared a single language at two different periods. We can also compare two languages to see the way in which they divide up a particular field. An often quoted example is that of colour terms. The Danish linguist Hjelmslev (1953: 33), argued that we could compare the

colour system of English and literary Welsh along a single
dimension (Figure 3). We shall discuss colour in more detail
in 4.3.

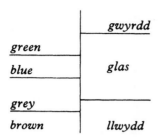

Figure 3

There are many other similar examples. Nida (1964: 50)
discusses, in terms of 'class', the words in a Mexican language for noise; there are six 'noise' words, referring to
children yelling, people talking loudly, people arguing (or
turkeys gobbling), people talking angrily, increasing noise
and funeral noise. Similarly he noted in Maya three words for
searching, (a) to select good from bad, (b) to search in a
disorderly way, (c) to search in an orderly way; and in Shilluk
(Africa) three 'break' words, one for breaking sticks, etc.,
one for string, one for eggs. We can add to this list a number
of familiar classes: the metals *iron*, *copper*, etc., the mammals
lion, *tiger*, etc., types of motor-car and so on.

In all these examples we have a list of words referring to
items of a particular class dividing up a semantic field. In
almost all cases, moreover, the words are INCOMPATIBLE. We
cannot say *This is a red hat* and of the same object *This is a
green hat*. Nor shall we allow a creature to be described both
as a lion and as an elephant. The incompatibility of terms
within a linguistic field is often clearly indicated in language.
Thus *It was on Saturday that she went there* implies that she
did not go there on Monday or any other day of the week (but
not that she did not go there in August), while *Bill púnched
Mary* (with contrastive stress) implies that he did not kick her

or slap her: *punch*, *kick* and *slap* all belong to the same
semantic field (Lyons 1977: 288). We can, however, recognise terms that seem to be mixtures: a hat can be orange-red,
while a tigon is the cross between a lion and a tiger. But by
introducing such terms we merely increase the words within
the field and divide the field up more finely. In some cases
the distinction between the terms in the field is clear, and
reflected by clear distinctions in experience; this is so, with
few exceptions, with the animal names. In other cases,
e.g. Nida's 'noise' words, the distinctions are far more
blurred.

Generally, too, the items in the field are 'unordered'; that
is to say there is no natural way, as far as their meaning is
concerned, of arranging them in any kind of order. If we
wanted to list them we should probably do so in alphabetic
order. Admittedly, the scientist will have a framework for the
classification of metals or mammals, but that is a different
matter; there is no way in which, in terms of an obvious
meaning characteristic, we can arrange *elephant*, *giraffe*, *rhi-
noceros*. But there are some groups of words that seem to have
some 'order'. The days of the week and the months of the
year form sets of incompatible items, for we cannot say *This
month is November and it is also March*. But they also have
sequential relations such that Sunday comes immediately
before Monday – *Sunday is the day before Monday*, etc. Similarly, measurements such as *inch*, *foot*, *yard* can be put in
order, starting from the smallest one. The numerals *one*, *two*,
three, etc., are another obvious example. Nida quotes a rather
different counting system from a Brazilian language in which
the terms are (roughly translated) 'none', 'one or two', 'three
or four', 'many'. The field is divided very differently from
the way in which it is divided in other languages, but the
basis of the sequencing, involving the notion of 'more than',
is clearly the same.

4.3 *Colour systems*

A whole section is devoted to colour here because, while it

has been handled in terms of field theory, it raises some interesting general problems of semantics.

We saw that Hjelmslev proposed a simple one-dimensional field that is said to be divided up differently by English and literary Welsh. He was thus able to place the colours in order. Yet this does not seem to be reflected in the language. We have no adjective to say that *Red is more — than orange* and *Orange is more — than yellow*, etc. The ordering is not reflected in English as is that of the days of the week or the months of the year. But if we are to look for the physical characteristics of colour, Hjelmslev's account says too little rather than too much. Colour is not to be accounted for in terms of a single dimension. It involves three variables. The most obvious is that of hue, which can be measured in wave-lengths and is seen in the spectrum or the rainbow. Another is luminosity or brightness and a third saturation, the degree of freedom from white. Thus *pink* differs from *red* mainly in that it has low saturation (it has a lot of white in it). We probably think of colour mainly as hue, but this may not be true of all societies. It has often been noted that Homer referred to the sea as 'wine-coloured', which is very odd if we think of its hue, but completely understandable if we think of its luminosity and saturation, which are very similar to those of a deep red wine.

It does not appear, however, that there is always a close relation between these physical features and the colour system of a particular language. Thus in a language of the Philippines, Hanunóo, described by Conklin (1955), there are four basic colour terms that may be roughly translated 'black', 'white', 'red' and 'green'. But the distinctions between them are of three kinds. First, light and dark essentially distinguishes 'black' and 'white' (all light tints being 'white', but violet, blue, dark green, being 'black'). Secondly, the distinction between 'red' and 'green' is largely in terms of the fact that all living plants are 'green', even slimy but light brown bamboo shoots. Thirdly, a distinction is made in terms of deep indelible colours 'black' and 'red' versus the weaker 'white' and 'green'. It is clear that the colour system is not solely based upon the physical features of colour, but is partly determined by the cultural needs, the need, for instance, to distinguish living and dead bamboo, one 'green' the other 'red'.

Even in English colour words are not always used in ways that correspond to their scientific definition. The use of *green* has some similarity to that found in Hanunóo, since dried peas are green in colour, but would not be referred to as *green peas*, while *green* is often used of unripe fruit – it may seem odd, but I should be understood, if I referred to some green-gages as being 'still green' and therefore inedible. Similarly (see 4.5), *white* is brown when relating to coffee, yellow when referring to wine and pink as applied to people. Modern Welsh, more surprisingly, has colour terms corresponding to those of English (not the older system described by Hjelmslev), yet uses the word *glas* to refer to grass and other growing things, though *glas* otherwise translates English *blue*.

Of course, some of these usages are rather specialised and a matter of particular collocations (see 4.4). The fact that I talk of *white coffee* does not suggest that I cannot use *white* in its stricter sense, any more than the fact that huntsmen refer to their bright red jackets as 'pink' suggests that they are colour-blind. Nevertheless, together with the observations of Hjelmslev and Conklin, we might well conclude that different languages deal with the field of colour in radically different ways.

A completely opposite view of colour terms is presented by Berlin & Kay (1969). On the basis of investigation into ninety-eight languages, with detailed research into twenty of them, they claim that there is a universal inventory of only eleven colour categories, from which all languages derive eleven or fewer basic colour terms. English has eleven – *white, black, red, green, yellow, blue, brown, purple, pink, orange* and *grey*. They also claim that there is a partial ordering of these categories, so that it can be predicted that, if a language has a certain colour term, it will have certain other ones. There is a simple rule:

$$
\begin{bmatrix} \text{white} \\ \\ \text{black} \end{bmatrix} < \text{[red]} < \begin{bmatrix} \text{green} \\ \\ \text{yellow} \end{bmatrix} < \text{[blue]} < \text{[brown]} < \begin{bmatrix} \text{purple} \\ \text{pink} \\ \text{orange} \\ \text{grey} \end{bmatrix}
$$

The sign < means that if a language has a term to the right it will have all the terms to the left. Thus, if it has 'green', it will have 'red', and, if it has 'brown', it will have 'blue'. Some of the terms are not ordered, but grouped together. In fact, all languages have 'black' and 'white', but some languages have 'green' without 'yellow' and others 'yellow' without 'green'. The last four colour terms usually occur together, although some languages have fewer than all four. The rule gives us a possible set of only twenty-two language types, though several of those that involve the last four terms are not attested. As examples, we are told that some languages of the New Guinea Highland group are Type 1 with only 'black' and 'white', while Plains Tamil (India) is Type 6 with 'white', 'black', 'red', 'green', 'yellow' and 'blue'. More recently Kay (1975) has slightly modified the system and the rule, to allow for 'grue' which combines 'green' and 'blue', but this is a matter of detail that does not affect the main argument. It is also suggested that we may set up seven evolutionary stages of language, according to the number of colour terms, and it is said that there is some evidence that children acquire colour terms in the same order.

Of course, if one language has only two or three colour terms, the range of each term is likely to be much wider than that of a language with the total of eleven. 'Black' will probably include all the dark reds, browns, greens, blues and purples, which the other languages will distinguish. This might seem to make it impossible to identify colours across languages and to support a view of the kind suggested by

Hjelmslev. But Berlin & Kay argue that their informants
were able to recognise not only the full range of each colour
term, but also its focus, the most typical example or examples
of the colours represented by the term. Thus, in a language
with three terms only, 'red' will spread over a much wider
area than that of *red* in English, but the foci will be very
similar; and we can thus establish, for all the languages, a set
of focal areas for the colour categories within which the foci
for the colour terms will be found. These generalised foci are,
moreover, discrete, except that there is a slight overlap for
'yellow' and 'orange' (Tzeltal and Cantonese 'yellow', Arabic
and Swahili 'orange'), and take up only a small part of the
total area of colour.

Berlin & Kay argue that colour categorisation in languages
is not random and that their results argue against any 'strict
relativity hypothesis' in favour of a 'weak universalist one'.
The notions of focus, of a limited set of basic terms and of
their partial ordering are clearly in direct conflict with any
view that says that colour is categorised arbitrarily in different languages.

Their claims are not accepted by all scholars. They themselves are aware of some counter-examples, e.g. that Russian
and Hungarian have twelve basic terms: Russian has two for
'blue' and Hungarian two for 'red'. There is also some question whether we really can distinguish BASIC colour terms
from other colour terms in a language, though they offer
some fairly plausible tests for this. There are problems with
the data too. Direct evidence was available for speakers of
only twenty languages and these, with one exception, all
lived around San Francisco and may well have adapted their
native systems to that of English or been influenced by
modern fashions in colour. In particular, it is even possible
that the measure of agreement concerning foci has resulted
from the world-wide use of modern synthetic dyes (McNeill
1972).

Nevertheless, there is enough evidence to suggest that
colour categorisation is not arbitrary and random and that we

are constrained, to some degree, to see colours as we do and so to label them in a somewhat consistent fashion. But we should not ignore the cultural relevance of colour categorisation. Even where languages have the 'same' terms, they may not apply them to exactly the same range of colours. Thus, the traditional Japanese 'red' and 'blue' would be *orange* and *turquoise* in English (because those were the colours of the vegetable dyes they used). Similarly, the Navaho system of basic colours 'white', 'black', 'red', 'blue-green' and 'yellow' is related to the use of objects and colours used in ceremonials (McNeill 1972).

Moreover, some colours are more obviously familiar in our experience. Red is the colour of blood, green of living plants, blue of the sky and the sea, and it would be curious, therefore, if a language lacked terms for these, but had a word for 'orange'.

Colour terminology is interesting and important in semantics because it is one of very few areas in which it is possible to compare a linguistic system with a system that can be both delimited and analysed in objective (physical) terms, though even here it must be conceded that the psychological recognition of colours may well not accord very closely with their physical characteristics. (Another area in which it is possible to compare the linguistic system with some kind of objective 'reality' is that of kinship; see 5.7.) This makes it possible to investigate the opposing claims of Hjelmslev and Berlin & Kay. It raises, as we have noted, the issue of the universality of semantic categories. We shall return to this in 5.8.

4.4 *Collocation*

Field theory as proposed by Trier is essentially concerned with paradigmatic relations. About the same time Porzig (1934) argued for the recognition of the importance of syntagmatic relations, between e.g. *bite* and *teeth*, *bark* and *dog*, *blond* and *hair*. In a slightly different way Firth (1951: 124[1957a: 195]; 1957b: 11[1968: 179]) argued that 'You shall know a word by the company it keeps.' His familiar example was that of *ass* which occurred (in a now defunct variety of English) in *You silly —, Don't be such an —* and with a limited set of adjectives such as *silly, obstinate, stupid, awful* and (occasionally!) *egregious*. For Firth this keeping company, which he called COLLOCATION, was part of the meaning of a word. As we have seen, meaning was also to be found in the context of situation and all the other levels of analysis as well.

It is, of course, obvious that by looking at the linguistic context of words we can often distinguish between different meanings. Nida (1964: 98), for instance, discussed the use of *chair* in:

(1) *sat in a chair*
(2) *the baby's high chair*
(3) *the chair of philosophy*
(4) *has accepted a University chair*
(5) *the chairman of the meeting*
(6) *will chair the meeting*
(7) *the electric chair*
(8) *condemned to the chair*

These are clearly in pairs, giving four different meanings of the word. But this does not so much establish, as illustrate, differences of meaning. Dictionaries, especially the larger ones, quite rightly make considerable use of this kind of contextualisation.

Collocation is not simply a matter of association of ideas. For, although milk is white, we should not often say *white milk*, though the expression *white paint* is common enough. Some of Porzig's examples seem more concerned with association of ideas. How often, one wonders, is *lick* actually collocated with *tongue*? More importantly, perhaps, although collocation is very largely determined by meaning, it is sometimes fairly idiosyncratic and cannot easily be predicted in terms of the meaning of the associated words. One example is Porzig's *blond* with *hair*. For we should not talk about **a* *blond door* or **a blond dress*, even if the colour were exactly that of blond hair. Similarly *rancid* occurs only with *bacon* and *butter*, and *addled* with *brains* and *eggs*, in spite of the fact that English has the terms *rotten* and *bad* and that *milk* never collocates with *rancid* but only with *sour*. We shall see (6.5) that *pretty child* and *buxom neighbour* would normally refer to females; here it is relevant to point out that we should not normally say *pretty boy* or *buxom man*, though *pretty girl* and *buxom woman* are quite normal. This characteristic of language is found in an extreme form in the collective words – *flock of sheep*, *herd of cows*, *school of whales*, *pride of lions*, and the rather more absurd examples such as *chattering of magpies*, *exaltation of larks*. Here we should also include *dog/bark*, *cat/mew*, *sheep/bleat*, *horse/neigh*, etc.

It is also the case that words may have more specific meanings in particular collocations. Thus we can speak of *abnormal* or *exceptional weather* if we have a heat wave in November, but *an exceptional child* is not an *abnormal child*, *exceptional* being used for greater than usual ability and *abnormal* to relate to some kind of defect (though, oddly, for 'euphemistic' reasons, *exceptional* is now being used by some people, especially in America, in place of *abnormal*).

It would, however, be a mistake to attempt to draw a clear distinguishing line between those collocations that are predictable from the meanings of the words that co-occur and those that are not (though some linguists have wished to restrict the term *collocation* to the latter). For one can, with varying degrees of plausibility, provide a semantic explanation for even the more restricted collocations, by assigning very particular meanings to the individual words. Thus it could be argued that *rancid* is to be defined in terms of the very specific, unpleasant, taste associated with butter and bacon that is 'off', that *pretty* describes only a feminine kind of beauty. We can also redefine our terms. We can thus explain *white coffee*, *white wine* and *white people* by suggesting that *white* means something like 'with the lightest of the normal colours associated with the entity'. There is some plausibility in accounting for *dogs bark*, *cats mew* in terms of the kind of noise made, since *bark* can also be used of other animals, e.g. squirrels. This should not, however, lead us to conclude that all of these restricted collocations can be accounted for semantically. For, not only is some of the semantic explanation a little implausible, but there are other examples where it would seem totally inappropriate. It is difficult to see any semantic explanation for the use of the collective terms. The only difference between *herd* and *flock* is that one is used with *cows* and the other with *sheep*.

In any case, it is often difficult, even in principle, to decide whether a collocation is or is not semantically determined, because the meaning of one of the collocated terms seems to depend upon the collocation. Thus Porzig (1934: 78) noted that the German verb *reiten* 'to ride' was originally restricted to riding a horse, but can now be used to denote sitting astride a beam. By contrast, the English verb *ride* is now used for riding a bicycle, but not sitting astride a beam (Lyons 1977: 263). We can see in these examples a widening of both the meaning and of the collocation, but it would be difficult to decide which of these two is the more basic. It might seem reasonable, at first, to say that the widening of the meaning has permitted the new collocation, but it is not obvious how the widened meanings can be stated except in terms of the new collocations – '*riding*' *the beam*, *riding a bicycle*.

Another difficulty that arises from any attempt to separate collocation and semantics is the fact that a word will often collocate with a number of other words that have something in common semantically. More strikingly (for negative examples often make the point more clearly), we find that individual words or sequences of words will NOT collocate with certain groups of words. Thus, though we may say *The rhododendron died*, we shall not say *The rhododendron passed away*, in spite of the fact that *pass away* seems to mean 'die'. But equally, of course, we should not use *pass away* with the names of any shrubs, not even with a shrub whose name we had heard for the first time. It is not very plausible to say that

pass away indicates a special kind of dying that is not characteristic of shrubs. It is rather that there is a restriction on its
use with a group of words that are semantically related. The
restrictions are, it has been suggested (McIntosh 1961), a
matter of RANGE; we know roughly the kind of nouns (in
terms of their meaning) with which a verb or adjective may
be used. So we do not reject specific collocations simply
because we have never heard them before – we rely on our
knowledge of the range.

We can, perhaps, see three kinds of collocational restriction. First, some are based wholly on the meaning of the item
as in the unlikely *green cow*. Secondly, some are based on
range – a word may be used with a whole set of words that
have some semantic features in common. This accounts for
the unlikeliness of *The rhododendron passed away* and equally
of *the pretty boy* (*pretty* being used with words denoting
females). Thirdly, some restrictions are collocational in the
strictest sense, involving neither meaning nor range, as
addled with *eggs* and *brains*. There are borderline cases. It
might be thought that *rancid* may be used with animal pro-
ducts of a certain type – perhaps *butter* and *bacon* have
something in common. But why not *rancid cheese* or *rancid
milk*?

4.5 *Idioms*

We cannot predict, for any given language, whether a particular meaning will be expressed by a single word or by a
sequence of words. Thus English PUNCH and KICK have to be
translated into French with *donner un coup de poing* and
donner un coup de pied. In these French examples we clearly
have instances of collocations that involve some association
of ideas, and the meaning of the entire expression can be
predicted from the meaning of the individual words.

Idioms involve collocation of a special kind. Consider, for
instance, *kick the bucket, fly off the handle, spill the beans, red
herring*. For here we not only have the collocation of *kick* and
the bucket, but also the fact that the meaning of the resultant

combination is opaque (2.4) – it is not related to the meaning
of the individual words, but is sometimes (though not always) nearer to the meaning of a single word (thus *kick the
bucket* equals *die*).

Although an idiom is semantically like a single word it does
not function like one. Thus we will not have a past tense
**kick the bucketed*. Instead, it functions to some degree as a
normal sequence of grammatical words, so that the past tense
form is *kicked the bucket*. But there are a great number of
grammatical restrictions. A large number of idioms contain a
verb and a noun, but although the verb may be placed in the
past tense, the number of the noun can never be changed. We
have *spilled the beans*, but not **spill the bean* and equally there
is no **fly off the handles*, **kick the buckets*, **put on good faces*,
**blow one's tops*, etc. Similarly, with *red herring* the noun may
be plural, but the adjective cannot be comparative (the *-er*
form). Thus we find *red herrings* but not **redder herring*.

There are also plenty of syntactic restrictions. Some
idioms have passives, but others do not. *The law was laid
down* and *The beans have been spilled* are all right (though
some may question the latter), but **The bucket was kicked* is
not. But in no case could we say *It was the —* (*beans that were
spilled*, *law that was laid down*, *bucket that was kicked*, etc.).
The restrictions vary from idiom to idiom. Some are more
restricted or 'frozen' than others.

A very common type of idiom in English is what is usually
called the 'phrasal verb', the combination of verb plus adverb
of the kind *make up*, *give in*, *put down*. The meaning of these
combinations cannot be predicted from the individual verb
and adverb and in many cases there is a single verb with the
same or a very close meaning – *invent*, *yield*, *quell*. Not all
combinations of this kind are idiomatic, of course. *Put down*
has a literal sense too and there are many others that are both
idiomatic and not, e.g. *take in* as in *The conjuror took the
audience in*, *The woman took the homeless children in*. There are
even degrees of idiomaticity since one can *make up* a story,
make up a fire or *make up* one's face. Moreover, it is not only

sequences of verb plus adverb that may be idiomatic. There are also sequences of verb plus preposition, such as *look after* and *go for*, and sequences of verb, adverb and preposition, such as *put up with* ('tolerate') or *do away with* ('kill').

There are also what we may call partial idioms, where one of the words has its usual meaning, the other has a meaning that is peculiar to the particular sequence. Thus *red hair* refers to hair, but not hair that is red in strict colour terms. Comedians have fun with partial idioms of this kind, e.g. when instructed to *make a bed* they bring out a set of carpenter's tools. Whether *white* in *white coffee*, *white wine* and *white people* is idiomatic depends on whether or not we define the term as 'with the lightest of the colours normally associated with the entity' (see 4.3, 4.4). Not surprisingly *black* is used as its opposite for coffee and people (though again neither are black in colour terms), yet it is not used for wine. Thus it can be seen that even partial idiomaticity can be a matter of degree and may in some cases be little more than a matter of collocational restriction. On a more comic level there is partial idiomaticity in *raining cats and dogs* (in Welsh it rains 'old women and sticks'!).

What is and what is not an idiom is, then, often a matter of degree. It is very difficult, moreover, to decide whether a word or a sequence of words is opaque. We could, perhaps, define idioms in terms of non-equivalence in other languages, so that *kick the bucket*, *red herring*, etc., are idioms because they cannot be directly translated into French or German. But this will not really work. The French for nurse is *garde-malade*, but while this cannot be directly translated into English it is quite transparent, obviously meaning someone who looks after the sick. On the other hand, *look after* seems quite idiomatic, yet it can be quite directly translated into Welsh (*edrych ar ôl*).

The problem of idioms is involved with the much wider issue of word formation, by which what would appear to be new and more complex lexemes can be formed from simpler ones. At one extreme we have expressions such as *public*

house, whose meaning is 'inn'. This is not a total idiom like
red herring, since the meaning can in part be related to *public*
and *house*, but one could certainly not predict from the words
themselves the existence of the compound. Then there are
words such as *blackbird* and *greenhouse* which are similarly
formed from other words, also without the possibility of
predicting that they could be formed with their particular
meanings. But the distinction between what is one word and
what is two is not wholly clear (see 2.4). Finally, there are the
derivatives, words formed by the use of suffixes, which differ
from the grammatical formations in that they are not regular,
either in formation or semantics. Thus we can contrast *boy/
boyish* with the purely grammatical *boy/boys*. Here, too, we
cannot predict that a form will exist with a certain meaning
for though we have *boyish*, *girlish*, *childish*, etc., there is no
*dogish or **catish*. Nor shall we find a constant meaning
associated with any one suffix. Chomsky (1970: 212) notes
that *readable* is more restricted in meaning than 'able to be
read' and that there are other restrictions with other words
ending in *-able* (*commendable*, *abominable*, *irreplaceable*, *in-
comparable*, *despicable*, *decidable*, *laudable*, *insufferable*,
noticeable, *changeable*, etc.).

   In all these cases there is a degree of idiomaticity. It might
be added, too, that even where we have transparency in
Ullmann's terms (see 2.4), there may still be some idiomaticity, though this depends on precisely what is meant by that
term. Consider again *chopper* (vs. *axe*) and German *Fingerhut*
(vs. *thimble*). There are two issues here. First, in neither case
can we predict that the form will occur (for we have no
transparent *-er* forms for *hammer* or *chisel*). Secondly, the
meaning is almost wholly predictable in *chopper*, but has to be
inferred or guessed in *Fingerhut*. The first issue is perhaps
more a matter of collocation, the latter of idiomaticity. This is
not, however, to say that we can make no generalisation
about the semantics of derivatives and compounds. On the
contrary, a great deal can be said; indeed books have been
written on the subject.

5

LEXICAL SEMANTICS: SENSE RELATIONS

In this chapter we shall be looking at some relations between words that are of a semi-logical kind, those that are, on a narrow interpretation, 'sense' relations. (For an excellent discussion see Lyons 1968.)

5.1 Some simple logic

Since some of the relations we are to consider are of a logical (or semi-logical kind) it would be useful to have some simple way of formalising them. This will be done in a simplified form of predicate calculus (see 6.6 and 8.3).

If we take a simple sentence such as *John is a man* we have a PREDICATION in which it is said of the individual John that he has the property of being a man. It is possible to symbolise this with $M(a)$, where M stands for the PREDICATE 'is a man' and a refers to the individual 'John'. We can extend this symbolism to deal with relations where more than one individual is concerned. Thus *John loves Mary* may be symbolised as $L(a,b)$, where L stands for the predicate ('loves') and a and b for 'John' and 'Mary'. The difference between this and the previous formula is that we have not one, but two, ARGUMENTS, a and b. It is important to add that the arguments are ORDERED, since *John loves Mary* ($L(a,b)$) is not the same as *Mary loves John* ($L(b,a)$). Other predicates may take even more arguments, e.g. *give* has three. Thus *John gave Mary a book* may be shown as $G(a,b,c)$.

The purpose of this symbolisation, however, is to show relations that hold between sentences (or propositions). Thus we might want to say that, if John is a bachelor, he is unmarried. This could be achieved by $B(a) \rightarrow U(a)$, where the

symbol → indicates ENTAILMENT, B stands for 'bachelor' and
U for 'unmarried', and the whole formula says that *John is a
bachelor* entails *John is unmarried*. However, since our purpose here would be to discuss the relation between *bachelor*
and *unmarried*, we want rather to say that for ANY individual,
not just John, being a bachelor entails being unmarried.
Instead of using *a*, *b* and *c* (INDIVIDUAL CONSTANTS), which
refer to specific individuals, we use the letters *x*, *y*, *z* as
INDIVIDUAL VARIABLES to refer to any individual and we
further introduce the Universal quantifier ∀ ('for all'). We can
now symbolise $\forall x\ (B(x) \rightarrow U(x))$, which is to be read 'For
all *x*, if *x* is a bachelor, *x* is unmarried'. We might further
wish to treat *unmarried* as 'not-married', and this can be
done by using the sign for negation, ∼: $\forall x\ (B(x) \rightarrow \sim M(x))$
(where M stands for 'married').

Where we have predicates with two or more arguments
(two- and many-place predicates), we can regard the predicates as expressing relations between the arguments. With
two-place predicates the relations may be characterised in
several ways, notably in terms of being SYMMETRIC, TRANSI-
TIVE and REFLEXIVE. A relation is symmetric if it holds for the
arguments in both directions, i.e. if for a relation R, it is the
case that $\forall x\ \forall y(R(x,y) \rightarrow R(y,x))$. Obvious examples in
English are *be married to* and *cousin*: if John is married to Mary,
Mary is married to John, and, if Bill is Fred's cousin, Fred is
Bill's cousin. A relation is transitive if, for three arguments *x*,
y and *z*, the relation that holds both for *x* and *y* and for *y* and
z, also holds for *x* and *z*, e.g. $\forall x\ \forall y\ \forall z(R(x,y)\ \&\ R(y,z)) \rightarrow
R(x,z)$. Many of the spatial terms are transitive – if John is in
front of Harry and Harry is in front of Bill, John is also in
front of Bill. The same is true for *behind*, *above*, *below*, *north
of*, *south of* and *inside*. This does not, of course, hold for
opposite, which is symmetrical (if No. 21 is opposite No. 22,
No. 22 is opposite No. 21), but not transitive. (It must be
noted that *transitive* and *transitivity* are used in a completely
different sense in grammar – see 6.4.) A relation is reflexive if
it relates an argument to itself, i.e. if $\forall x\ (R(x,x))$. It can be

exemplified by *equal* or *resemble* (*Four equals four, John resembles himself*). (These words express relations that are symmetric and transitive too.) Reflexivity is, however, of little interest to us here, and will not be further discussed.

Relations that can never be symmetric, transitive or reflexive are ASYMMETRIC, INTRANSITIVE and IRREFLEXIVE respectively. A relation that is all three of these is that of *father of* since (1) if *x* is father of *y*, *y* cannot be father of *x*, (2) if, in addition, *y* is father of *z*, *x* cannot be father of *z*, (3) *x* cannot be father of *x*. Notice however, that a relation that is not symmetric, transitive or reflexive (e.g. *like*) is not necessarily asymmetric, intransitive or irreflexive. For (1) if *x* likes *y*, *y* may (or may not) like *x*, (2) if, in addition, *y* likes *z*, *x* may (or may not) like *z*, (3) *x* may (or may not) like *x*.

5.2 *Hyponymy*

In 4.2 we discussed classes or sets of incompatible items. But there are also words that refer to the class itself. HYPONYMY involves us in the notion of INCLUSION in the sense that *tulip* and *rose* are included in *flower*, and *lion* and *elephant* in *mammal* (or perhaps *animal* – see below). Similarly *scarlet* is included in *red*. Inclusion is thus a matter of class membership. The 'upper' term is the SUPERORDINATE and the 'lower' term the HYPONYM.

In 4.2 we were concerned with members of a class, with, that is to say, co-hyponyms. Yet oddly there is not always a superordinate term. Lyons (1963: 70–1) observed that in Classical Greek there is a superordinate term to cover a variety of professions and crafts, 'carpenter', 'doctor', 'flute player', 'helmsman', 'shoemaker', etc., but none in English. The nearest possible term is *craftsman*, but that would not include *doctor*, *flute player* or *helmsman*. Similarly, and rather strangely, there is no superordinate term for all colour words, *red*, *blue*, *green*, *white*, etc.; the term *coloured* usually excludes *black* and *white* (and *grey* too), or else (used to refer to race), means 'non-white'.

The same term may appear in several places in the

hierarchy. This is, of course, possible only if it is polysemic (has several meanings – see 5.6); in one of its meanings it may actually be superordinate to itself in another meaning (though we should usually avoid using both terms in the same context). Thus *animal* may be used (1) in contrast with *vegetable* to include birds, fishes, insects as well as mammals, (2) in the sense of 'mammal' to contrast with birds, fishes and insects, to include both humans and beasts, (3) in the sense of 'beast' to contrast with *human*. Thus it occurs three times in the hierarchical classification of nature. Figure 4 illustrates the point clearly:

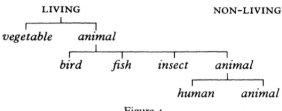

Figure 4

There is a similar situation with the word *dog*. The word *sheep* is used for all creatures of a certain species; it is the superordinate term of *ewe*, *lamb*, *ram*, etc. There are similar terms *pig* for *sow*, *boar*, *piglet* and *horse* for *stallion*, *mare*, *colt*, etc. But the superordinate term for dogs is *dog*, though *dog* is also the hyponym as distinct from *bitch*. Figure 5 will help. We can, of course, avoid the ambiguity of *dog* by using the term *male*; *male dog* would be the hyponym to contrast with *bitch*. We can also form hyponymous sets where no single-word hyponyms exist in English in a similar way, e.g. *giraffe*, *male giraffe*, *female giraffe*, *baby giraffe*. The terms *cattle* and *poultry* are a little odd in that, though they are superordinate,

```
        sheep                    dog
   ┌──────┼──────┐         ┌──────┼──────┐
  ram   ewe   lamb        dog   bitch  puppy
```

Figure 5

they are used only for plural reference (though, of course, we need the superordinate term quite commonly for the plural). Thus, though we may say *Those are cattle* to include *Those are cows*, *Those are bulls*, we have no single term to put in the frame *That is a —*. The most likely term here would be *cow*. (We might find it difficult to say *That is a cow* of a bull, but would not be unhappy with the definition of a bull as *a male cow*.) With *poultry* the situation seems to vary according to interest and dialect. The terms *cock* (or *cockerel* and, in America, *rooster*), *hen* and *chick* are available, but many people use *hen* or *chicken* as the superordinate term, though would not, I suspect, ever wish to refer to the male bird as a *hen*. In my own native dialect there is no problem – the superordinate term is *fowl*.

As we might expect, hyponymy relations vary from language to language. We have seen one example – that Greek has a superordinate term to include a variety of occupations. Another example is that in German 'potato' *Kartoffel* is not included among 'vegetables' *Gemüse*.

Hyponymy involves entailment. To say *This is a tulip* entails *This is a flower*, and *This is scarlet* entails *This is red*. We can formalise the relation between *tulip* and *flower* as $\forall x(T(x) \rightarrow F(x))$, though such a formula by itself will not bring out the hierarchical classification involved in hyponymy, for since a tulip and a flower are also plants, we can say $\forall x(T(x) \rightarrow P(x))$ and $\forall x(F(x) \rightarrow P(x))$, but it must not follow from this that *tulip* and *flower* are both co-hyponyms of *plant*. We need further to specify that *flower* is an IMMEDIATE hyponym of *plant* and that *tulip* is an IMMEDIATE hyponym of *flower*.

This kind of analysis forms the basis of Carnap's (1956) MEANING POSTULATES, where it is suggested that the meaning of lexical items can be stated in terms of such entailments. Thus, as we saw, *x is a bachelor* entails *x is unmarried* ($\forall x(B(x) \rightarrow \sim M(x))$). In this sense, of course, *being a bachelor* is hyponymous to *being unmarried*. Meaning postulates thus essentially treat hyponymy as the basic sense relation.

5.3 *Synonymy*

SYNONYMY is used to mean 'sameness of meaning'. It is
obvious that for the dictionary-maker many sets of words
have the same meaning; they are synonymous, or are
synonyms of one another. This makes it possible to define
gala as *festivity* or *mavis* as *thrush*, though there is little use in
this method if neither word is known to the reader, e.g. if
hoatzin is defined as *stink-bird*; or *neve* as *firn*. Of course,
dictionaries seldom rely solely on synonymy, but add descriptive details to enlighten the reader. We can, in fact,
define synonymy as symmetric hyponymy. Thus, if *mavis*
and *thrush* are synonymous, we can say $\forall x(M(x) \rightarrow T(x))$ and
$\forall x(T(x) \rightarrow M(x))$, i.e. that all mavises are thrushes and all
thrushes are mavises. But this does not solve the many
practical problems that we must face.

It has often been suggested that English is particularly rich
in synonyms for the historical reason that its vocabulary has
come from two different sources, from Anglo-Saxon on the
one hand and from French, Latin and Greek on the other.
Since English is considered to be a Germanic language from a
historical point of view, with Anglo-Saxon as an earlier stage
of its development, the 'Anglo-Saxon' words are often considered to be 'native' while those from French, Latin or Greek
are 'foreign', 'borrowed' from these languages. But the terms
'native' and 'foreign' are misleading. For whatever their
origins, most of the words are an essential and wholly natural
part of the English language; moreover, even some of the
'native' words may well have been 'borrowed' from some
other language at some time in the more remote past. Unfortunately, there are often moves to remove the 'foreign' element from languages. Frenchmen deplore 'Franglais' (the
English words that are now common in colloquial French),
while the Welsh spend time and scholarship to find substi-
tutes for the 'English' words in the language, though they are
quite happy to retain the 'Latin' words that entered an earlier
form of the language at the time of the Roman Empire.

Nevertheless, it is true that there are pairs of 'native' and 'foreign' words. Thus we have *brotherly* and *fraternal*, *buy* and *purchase*, *world* and *universe*, and many others. The 'native' words are often shorter and less learned; four-letter words (in the quite literal sense) are mostly from Anglo-Saxon. There are examples too of triples, one 'native', one from French, one directly from Latin – *kingly*, *royal*, *regal* (though with this set it is the word of French origin, *royal*, that is today in more common usage).

It can, however, be maintained that there are no real synonyms, that no two words have exactly the same meaning. Indeed it would seem unlikely that two words with exactly the same meaning would both survive in a language. If we look at possible synonyms there are at least five ways in which they can be seen to differ.

First, some sets of synonyms belong to different dialects of the language. For instance, the term *fall* is used in the United States and in some western counties of Britain where others would use *autumn*. The works of dialectologists are full of examples like these. They are especially interested in the words to do with farming; depending where you live you will say *cowshed*, *cowhouse* or *byre*, *haystack*, *hayrick* or *haymow*. Even the domestic *tap* is either a *faucet* or a *spigot* in most of the United States. But these groups of words are of no interest at all for semantics. Their status is no different from the translation-equivalents of, say, English and French. It is simply a matter of people speaking different forms of the language having different vocabulary items.

Secondly, there is a similar situation, but a more problematic one, with the words that are used in different styles (3.5). *A nasty smell* might be, in the appropriate setting, *an obnoxious effluvium* or *an 'orrible stink*. The former is, of course, jocularly very 'posh', and the latter colloquial. Similar trios (though not with quite the same stylistic characteristics, but differing rather in degrees of formality) are *gentleman*, *man* and *chap*, *pass away*, *die* and *pop off*. These are more difficult to deal with because there is a far less clear distinction between the styles than between the geographically defined dialects and, as we saw in 3.5, there is a theoretical problem whether such stylistic differences should be regarded as within semantics or treated as features of different 'languages'.

Thirdly, some words may be said to differ only in their emotive or evaluative meanings. The remainder of their meaning, their 'cognitive' meaning, remains the same. Some semanticists have made a great play with the emotive difference between *politician* and *statesman*, *hide* and *conceal*, *liberty* and *freedom*, each implying approval or disapproval. The function of such words in language is, of course, to influence attitudes. There are far more subtle ways than saying something is good or bad or even of choosing a 'good' or a 'bad' word. In politics particular words are often chosen simply for the effect they are likely to have. *Fascist* no longer refers to a member of the fascist parties, it is simply used to condemn and insult opponents. Words may have different emotive meanings in different societies. On the whole *liberal* is a 'good' word in Great Britain – even used by Winston Churchill of himself when he was politically a Conservative, but it is a 'bad' word in South Africa and in some political circles in the United States. Nevertheless, it is a mistake to attempt to separate such emotive or evaluative meaning from the 'basic' 'cognitive' meaning of words for three reasons. First, it is not easy to establish precisely what cognitive meaning is, and certainly not reasonable to attempt to define it in terms of reference to physical properties. On such a definition, most verbs and adjectives would have little or no cognitive meaning. Secondly, there are words in English that are used PURELY for evaluative purposes, most obviously the adjectives *good* and *bad*, but it is not normally assumed that they have no cognitive meaning. Such words are of interest to moral philosophers, but should not, I believe, have any special place in linguistics. Thirdly, we make all kinds of judgments and do not merely judge in terms of 'good' and 'bad'. We judge size and use the appropriate terms – *giant/dwarf*, *mountain/hill*, etc., and we make other kinds of judgments in our choice of words. The meaning of words is not simply a matter of objective facts; a great deal of it is subjective and we cannot clearly distinguish between the two.

Fourthly, some words are collocationally restricted (see 4.4), i.e. they occur only in conjunction with other words. Thus *rancid* occurs with *bacon* or *butter*, *addled* with *eggs* or *brains*. This does not seem to be a matter of their meaning, but of the company they keep. It could, perhaps, be argued that these are true synonyms – differing only in that they occur in different environments.

Fifthly, it is obviously the case that many words are close in meaning, or that their meanings overlap. There is, that is to say, a loose sense of synonymy. This is the kind of synonymy that is exploited by the dictionary-maker. For *mature* (adjective), for instance, possible synonyms are *adult*, *ripe*, *perfect*, *due*. For *govern* we may suggest *direct*, *control*, *determine*, *require*, while *loose* (adjective) will have an even larger set – *inexact*, *free*, *relaxed*, *vague*, *lax*, *unbound*, *inattentive*, *slack*, etc. If we look for the synonyms for each of these words themselves, we shall have a further set for each and shall, of course, get further and further away from the meaning of the original word. Dictionaries, unfortunately (except the very large ones), tell us little about the precise connections between words and their defining synonyms or between the synonyms themselves.

It would be useful if we had some way of testing synonymy. One way, perhaps, is substitution – substituting one word for another. It has been suggested that true or total synonyms are mutually interchangeable in all their environments. But it is almost certainly the case that there are no total synonyms in this sense; indeed this would seem to be a corollary of the belief that no two words have exactly the same meaning. What we shall find, of course, is that some words are interchangeable in certain environments only, e.g. that *deep* or *profound* may be used with *sympathy* but only *deep* with *water*, that a *road* may be *broad* or *wide* but an *accent* only *broad*. But this will give us little measure of synonymy or of similarity of meaning; it will merely indicate the collocational possibilities, and these do not seem necessarily to be always closely related to nearness of meaning.

Another possibility is to investigate the 'opposites' (the antonyms, to be discussed in 5.4). Thus *superficial* is to be contrasted with both *deep* and *profound*, but *shallow* is, for the most part, in contrast only with *deep*. Perhaps the fact that two words appear to have the same antonyms is a reason for treating them as synonyms, but the examples we have just discussed show that we shall again arrive at the words that are interchangeable in certain environments, for it is precisely in the context in which *deep* and *profound* are interchangeable that they have the antonym *superficial*.

Synonyms are often said to differ only in their CONNOTA-TIONS. This is not a very useful term. It often refers to emotive or evaluative meaning which, I have argued, is not usefully distinguished from cognitive meaning. It is also used to refer to stylistic or even dialectal differences or even to the small differences that are found in near-synonyms. But there is a further rather interesting use. It is sometimes suggested that words become associated with certain characteristics of the items to which they refer. Thus *woman* has the connota-tion 'gentle' and *pig* the connotation 'dirty'. Such connota-tions were the subject of Osgood's investigations (1.4). Strictly, however, this is not a matter of the meaning of words or even of meaning in general. It rather indicates that people (or some people) believe that women are gentle and pigs dirty. It is true that people will change names in order to avoid such connotations, and there is a natural process of change with taboo words such as those mentioned in 1.3. Because the word is associated with a socially distasteful subject, it becomes distasteful itself, and another word, a 'euphemism', takes its place. But the process is, of course, unending since it is essentially the object and not the word that is unpleasant. Words even become taboo when the dis-tasteful object is referred to by the word in a different sense (whether it is homonymous or polysemous – see 5.6). Thus we are unwilling to talk of *intercourse* to mean social or commercial relationships, and it has been often pointed out that it is for similar reasons that in America the male domestic fowl is a *rooster*.

There are two phenomena that are sometimes handled under synonymy that have not yet been considered in this section. The first is context-dependent synonymy where two items appear to be synonymous in a particular context. Examples are *dog* and *bitch* in *My — has just had pups* and *buy* and *get* in *I'll go to the shop and — some bread* (Lyons 1968: 452–3). But this does not seem to be an argument for the synonymy of the words. On the contrary they are related in terms of hyponymy (see 5.2), one term being more specific than the other. The context, however, supplies the specific information that is lacking in one of the examples: having pups indicates that the dog is female, going to the shop suggests that the bread is to be bought. But this is not part of the meaning. The dog might not be female (remarkable though it would be), and I might steal the bread. The fact that information can be gleaned from the context does not affect the meaning of items. For consider *the book* and *the red book*. These could well be contextually synonymous (if we had already mentioned a red book – or, non-linguistically, if there was one, red, book before us). Yet we should not wish to say that these have the same meaning. The second kind of 'synonymy' is that between *bull* and *male adult bovine animal*. The test of interchangeability would rule these out completely as synonymous, for one would hardly say *There is a male adult bovine animal in the field*, even though in some sense the two items seem to have the same meaning. But this is not a natural linguistic phenomenon; it is created by the linguist or lexicographer for the purposes of definition and paraphrase. It relates, moreover, more to componential analysis (5.7) than to synonymy.

5.4 *Antonymy*

The term ANTONYMY is used for 'oppositeness of meaning';
words that are opposite are ANTONYMS. Antonymy is often
thought of as the opposite of synonymy, but the status of the
two are very different. For languages have no real need of
true synonyms, and, as we have seen, it is doubtful whether
any true synonyms exist. But antonymy is a regular and very
natural feature of language and can be defined fairly precisely. Yet, surprisingly, it is a subject that has often been
neglected in books on semantics and it is not even usually
given a place in dictionaries. However, there are different
kinds of 'oppositeness' and we must clearly distinguish them.

   To begin with, English abounds in pairs of words such as
wide/narrow, *old/young*, *big/small*, etc. These, all of them
adjectives, have in common the fact that they may be seen in
terms of degrees of the quality involved. Thus a road may be
wide or *very wide* and one road may be *wider* than another.
We have, that is to say, gradation of width, age, size, etc., all
indicated by such adjectives as these.

   Sapir (1944 [1949]) argued that we should handle all these
words in terms of GRADING. The comparative forms of the
adjectives (those ending in -*er* or occurring with *more*) are
EXPLICITLY graded, since to say that one road is wider than
another, one boy is older than another or one book is bigger
than another is to place them in a graded scale for comparison. Sapir went on to argue that although these comparative
forms are preceded linguistically by the simple forms (i.e.
formed from them by adding -*er* or *more*), they precede them
logically in that *wide*, *old* and *big* can only be understood in
terms of being wider, older, bigger than something – some
norm or other. They are thus, said Sapir, IMPLICITLY graded
antonyms.

   Not only are these adjectives gradable, but they are graded
against different norms according to the items being discussed. For instance, if I say that not many people were
present, this might mean five or six if we were talking about

an intimate party, but perhaps as many as twenty thousand if we were talking about the attendance at an important football match at Wembley. The norm is set by the object being described. A stripe on a dress may be wide if it is only two inches wide, but a road would have to be many yards wide before it could be so described. This accounts for the apparent paradox of a small elephant being bigger than a big mouse for *small* means 'small as elephants go' and *big* 'big as mice go'.

For most antonyms a set of relationships hold between the comparative forms such that all of the following are mutually implied:

> *The road is wider than the lane.*
> *The lane is narrower than the road.*
> *The road is less narrow than the lane.*
> *The lane is less wide than the road.*

These are related both in terms of simple reversal with switch of antonyms, and the 'more' and 'less' relationship (again involving switch of antonyms). Not surprisingly, since antonyms are gradable, there are often intermediate terms. Thus we have not just *hot/cold*, but *hot/warm/cool/cold*, with the intermediate *warm* and *cool* forming a pair of antonyms themselves.

A further point is that in each pair one of the terms is the MARKED term and the other UNMARKED in that only one is used simply to ask about or describe the degree of the gradable quality. We say *How high is it? How wide is it? It is three feet high*, *It is four yards wide*, with no implication that it is either high or wide. But the other term of the pair is not so used – it is the marked term. Thus *How low is it? How narrow is it?* imply that the object in question actually is low or narrow and we would not say (except jocularly) **It is three feet low* or **It is four yards narrow*. Notice also that the same member of the pair is used to form the nouns, *height* and *width*, which are equally neutral as compared with *lowness* and *narrowness*. In the English examples it is the 'larger' term that appears to be unmarked, but this does not appear to be a universal feature. Where English talks of a *thickness gauge*, Japanese talks of a 'thinness gauge'.

We may, perhaps, also include here pairs of the type *male/female*, *married/single*, *alive/dead*. These Lyons (1968: 460) treats in term of COMPLEMENTARITY, the items being complementary to each other. Strictly these belong to the set of incompatible terms that were discussed in 4.2, but with one specific characteristic – that they are members of two-term sets instead of the multiple-term sets that we discussed there. But they are in some ways similar to our gradable antonyms. Both exhibit incompatibility. To say that something is wide is to say that it is not narrow. To say that someone is married is to say that he is not single. But there is one striking difference between the two types. With the pairs we have introduced it is also the case that to say something is NOT the one is to say that it is the other. If Peter is NOT married, he is single, and vice versa. This results, of course, from the fact that there are only two possibilities (it would not be the same with the multiple sets). With the gradable antonyms, in contrast, although there are only two terms, it is not the case that to say something is not (for instance) wide is to say that it is narrow, or that to say it is not narrow is to say that it is wide. The possibility of being neither wide nor narrow is left open.

Antonyms and complementaries do not lend themselves very easily to the kind of logical formalisation suggested earlier. For antonyms we wish to say that if something is A it is not B (and vice versa), while for complementaries we have to say, in addition, that if it is not A it is B (and vice versa). Thus for the antonyms *wide* and *narrow* we have $\forall x(W(x) \rightarrow \sim N(x))$ and $\forall x(N(x) \rightarrow \sim W(x))$ (though this follows logically), while for the complementaries *male* and *female* the formulae are $\forall x(M(x) \rightarrow \sim F(x))$ and $\forall x(\sim M(x) \rightarrow F(x))$ together with $\forall x(F(x) \rightarrow \sim M(x))$ and $\forall x(\sim F(x) \rightarrow M(x))$ (which also follow from the first two). But this is not sufficient to characterise complementaries and antonyms. In both cases we must also show that they belong to the same semantic system or field (4.2). For, to take complementaries first, it is not true to say that, if something is not male, it is female, since it could also be inanimate. The complementarity of *male* and *female* is restricted to the discussion of animates. Similarly, we should not regard *simian* and *ferrous* as antonyms, in spite of the fact that if something is a monkey it is not iron (and vice versa). Moreover, with antonyms it is not enough that the terms also belong to the same system. For *equine* and *bovine* are not antonyms. The notion of gradability is also essential.

A further interesting point is that there is no absolute distinction between these two types. We can treat *male/ female*, *married/single*, *alive/dead* as gradable antonyms on occasions. Someone can be *very male* or *more married* and certainly *more dead than alive*. More obviously, some gradable antonyms have some characteristics of the dichotomous pairs:

(1) There are some pairs of adjectives, e.g. *honest/dishonest*, *obedient/disobedient*, *open/shut* that are gradable in terms of *more* and *less*, yet in which the denial of one is usually taken to assert the other. Thus though we may say *Bill is more honest than John*, *Bill isn't honest* implies that *Bill is dishonest*, and *Bill isn't dishonest* implies that *Bill is honest*. These are, that is to say, explicitly gradable, but they are not usually treated as implicitly gradable.

(2) Some pairs of antonyms are, in Sapir's terms, not 'symmetrically reversible'. That is to say the *more* and *less* relationship cannot be applied to them. An example is the pair *brilliant* and *stupid*, since *more brilliant* does not equal *less stupid* or *more stupid*, *less brilliant*. The terms, though gradable, also have an absolute value at one of the 'ends' of the scale.

5.5 *Relational opposites*

A quite different kind of 'opposite' is found with pairs of words which exhibit the reversal of a relationship between items (or ARGUMENT – see 5.1). Examples are *buy/sell, husband/wife*. If John sells to Fred, Fred buys from John; if Bill is Mary's husband, Mary is Bill's wife. Lyons (1968: 467) suggests the term CONVERSENESS for these, but I am more concerned to point out their essentially relational characteristics, and would thus prefer RELATIONAL OPPOSITION.

There are several verbs that are pairs in this way – *buy/sell, lend/borrow, rent/let, own/belong to, give/receive*. There are also nouns – *husband/wife, fiancé/fiancée, parent/child, debtor/creditor*, and, possibly, *teacher/pupil*. A number of terms referring to spatial position also belong here – *above/below, in front of/behind, north of/south of*, etc. In grammar, too, active and passive exhibit relational opposition, for if Tom hits Harry, Harry is hit by Tom.

Terms involved in relational opposition may be transitive, e.g. both *above* and *below*. If the picture is above the table and the table above the carpet, the picture is above the carpet (and similarly for *below*). They cannot, of course, be symmetric, for symmetric relations are those in which, by definition, the same relation holds between the arguments in both directions, so that only one term, not two, is required. Whereas relational opposites involve two relations R and R' such that $\forall x \forall y(R(x,y) \rightarrow R'(y,x))$, symmetric relations involve only one, such that $\forall x \forall y(R(x,y) \rightarrow R(y,x))$. Examples of terms in a symmetric relationship are *married to, beside, meet*.

Kinship terms are especially interesting in a discussion of relational opposites for two reasons. In the first place many of them indicate not only the relationship, but the sex of the person concerned. Thus *father* is the male parent, *daughter* a female child and so on. This blocks reversibility. For to say that John is Sam's father does not entail that Sam is John's son – Sam could be his daughter. We therefore have pairs indicating the same relationship but a different sex: *father/ mother, son/daughter, uncle/aunt, nephew/niece*. There are also pairs of words that would be symmetric were it not for their indication of sex. An example are *brother* and *sister*. It does not follow that if John is Sam's brother, Sam is John's brother (she might be his sister). Only a small number of terms in English do not indicate sex – *cousin* (which is symmetric) and *parent* and *child*, together with *grandparent* and *grandchild* (which are not). There are other terms that avoid sex reference and so are symmetric, but are mostly used only by anthropologists – *spouse* for *husband/wife* and *sibling* for *brother/sister*. But there are no similar terms for *uncle/aunt*, *nephew/niece*. Secondly, whether a term is symmetric or not is a matter of the language. Thus *be married to* is symmetric in English because, like *spouse*, it does not indicate sex. But in many languages a different term is used for husband and wife, quite often the active form of the verb for the husband and the passive term for the wife – John 'marries' Mary but Mary 'is married' to John. (In English *marry* and *be married to* are used for either partner, and so are both symmetric.) Similarly, many languages have no symmetric term *cousin*; the sex has to be indicated in these languages, or the precise relationship of the parents. There may be other complications too. The brother and sister relationship in some languages is bound up not only with the sex, but also the age of the child; thus if two girls are sisters, one is the 'elder sister', one the 'younger sister' of the other.

There are some other terms that are not strictly related as relational opposites, but nevertheless differ in spatial direction in some way. We have already discussed *come* and *go* (3.5), and there are other pairs of words that seem to be related in similar ways. Thus *ask* expects *reply* and *offer*, *accept*. These are not examples of relational opposites, but of a temporal relationship. Moreover the relationship between the members of each pair is not the same. *Ask* and *offer* may 'expect' *reply* and *accept*, but the 'expectation' may be disappointed – there may be no reply or acceptance (though, for *offer*, there is also the term *refuse*). But *reply* and *accept* also 'presuppose' that there has been an act of asking or giving (see 7.4); this is a natural result of the temporal relationship.

Finally, it is worth noting that the 'true' gradable

antonyms can be handled in terms of relational opposites. For we saw that *wide* can be seen as wider than the norm and that if *a* is wider than *b*, *b* is narrower than *a*. The comparative forms *wider* and *narrower* (the explicitly gradable forms) are thus relational opposites; they are, moreover, transitive (if *a* is wider than *b* and *b* is wider than *c*, *a* is wider than *c*), but not symmetric or reflexive. Notice, however, that *as wide as*, *as narrow as*, etc., are symmetric, transitive and reflexive.

5.6 *Polysemy and homonymy*

Sameness of meaning is not very easy to deal with but there seems nothing inherently difficult about difference of meaning. Not only do different words have different meanings; it is also the case that the same word may have a set of different meanings. This is POLYSEMY; such a word is POLYSEMIC. Thus the dictionary will define the word *flight* in at least the following ways: 'passing through the air', 'power of flying', 'air journey', 'unit of the Air Force', 'volley', 'digression', 'series of steps'. Yet there are problems even with this apparently simple concept.

To begin with, we cannot clearly distinguish whether two meanings are the same or different and, therefore, determine exactly how many meanings a word has. For a meaning is not easily delimited and so distinguished from other meanings. Consider the verb *eat*. The dictionary will distinguish the 'literal' sense (see below) of taking food and the derived meanings of 'use up' and 'corrode' and we should, perhaps, treat these as three different meanings. But we can also distinguish between eating meat and eating soup, the former with a knife and fork and the latter with a spoon. Moreover, we can talk about drinking soup as well as eating it. In one of its senses, then, *eat* corresponds to *drink*. The problem, however, is to decide whether this represents a distinct meaning of *eat*; for an alternative solution is that the meaning of *eat* merely overlaps that of *drink*, but that each covers a wide semantic 'area' (a great deal of which does not overlap). If we decide, however, that there are two meanings of *eat*, we may then ask whether eating jelly is the same thing as eating toffee (which involves chewing) or eating sweets (which involves sucking). Clearly we eat different types of food in different ways, and, if we are not careful, we shall decide that the verb *eat* has a different meaning with every type of food that we eat. The moral is that we ought not to look for all possible differences of meaning, but to look for sameness of meaning as far as we can, and to accept that there is no clear criterion of either difference or sameness.

A more practical problem is that if one form has several meanings, it is not always clear whether we shall say that this is an example of polysemy (that there is one word with several meanings) or of HOMONYMY (that there are several words with the same shape). For instance we noted earlier that the dictionary treats *flight* as a single (polysemic) word. But it recognises no less than five words (i.e. five homonyms) for *mail* – 'armour', 'post', 'halfpenny', 'payment' and 'spot' (the third meaning is shown as 'obsolete' and the last two are 'Scottish', but the important point is that they are not shown as different meanings of the same word). The dictionary has to decide whether a particular item is to be handled in terms of polysemy or homonymy, because a polysemic item will be treated as a single entry, while a homonymous one will have a separate entry for each of the homonyms. This does not mean, of course, that we can decide between polysemy and homonymy merely by consulting the dictionary, for we must question the reasons for the decisions made by the dictionary-maker and, in some cases, these seem to be quite arbitrary.

There is some complication in the fact that we do not make the same distinctions in writing and speech. Thus *lead* (metal) and *lead* (dog's lead) are spelt in the same way, but pronounced differently, while *site* and *sight*, *rite* and *right* are spelt differently but pronounced in the same way. For the former the term HOMOGRAPHY may be used, for the latter HOMOPHONY. Curiously there are some homonyms and homophones that are also (very nearly) antonyms, e.g. *cleave* 'part asunder' and *cleave* 'unite' and *raise* and *raze*.

The problem, however, is to decide when we have polysemy and when we have homonymy. Given that we have a written form with two meanings, are we to say that it is one word with different meanings (polysemy) or two different words with the same shape (homonymy)? There are a number of possible ways of answering this question. First, dictionaries usually base their decision upon etymology. If it is known that identical forms have different origins they are treated as homonymous and given separate entries; if it is known that they have one origin, even if they have different meanings, they are treated as polysemic and given a single entry in the dictionary. This is, however, far from satisfactory, for the history of a language does not always reflect accurately its present state. For instance, we should not usually relate *pupil* (=student) with the *pupil* of the eye, or the *sole* of a shoe with the fish *sole*. Yet historically they are from the same origin, and as such are examples of polysemy. Yet in the language of today they are pairs of unrelated words, i.e. homonyms. On the other side we find that we speak of the *hands* and *face* of a clock, the *foot* of a bed or of a mountain, the *leg* of a chair or table, the *tongue* of a shoe, the *eye* of a needle or a potato, as well as using the same terms for parts of the body, and similarly have the word *ear* used of the *ear* of corn. These would all seem to be examples of metaphor and, so, of polysemy. Yet the etymologists tell us that the *ear* of corn is in no way related (historically) to the *ear* of the body. Historically, then, they are homonyms. But most people today would regard them as the same word with different meanings, i.e. as examples of polysemy. There are other examples – *corn* (=grain) and *corn* on the foot, *meal* (=repast) and *meal* (=flour), each of which has a different etymology. But are they different words for us today? History can be misleading.

Curiously, a difference of spelling does not always indicate a difference of origin. Thus even what are today homophones may be derived from the same original form. Examples are *metal* and *mettle*, *flour* and *flower*. These pose real problems for the semanticist. For if he relies on his historical knowledge, they are the same word, merely examples of polysemy, even though they are spelt differently. Yet this is odd. Can we consider words that are spelt differently to be the 'same' word? Yet we find that difference of spelling does not guarantee difference of origin. Does the dictionary-maker then treat these as different words because they are spelt differently, or as the same word because they have a single origin? In practice he usually (but not always) allows the spelling difference to decide, because he needs to keep words in their alphabetical position.

Secondly, we may ask whether we can make any general remarks about difference of meaning. Are regular types of difference found in the meaning of various words? For it is reasonable to suggest that where the differences are regular and to some degree predictable, we have polysemy rather than homonymy. One of the most familiar kinds of relationships between meanings is that of METAPHOR where a word appears to have both a 'literal' meaning and one or more 'transferred' meanings. The most striking set of examples is found with the words for parts of the body, *hand*, *foot*, *face*, *leg*, *tongue*, *eye*, etc. Intuitively it is clear enough which is the literal sense, and our intuitions are supported by the fact that the whole set of words applies only to the body; only some of them can be transferred to the relevant object – the clock has no legs, the bed no hands, the chair no tongue, etc.

Metaphor is, however, fairly haphazard. It may seem obvious that *foot* is appropriate to mountains, or *eye* to needles, but a glance at other languages shows that it is not. In French the needle does not have an 'eye', and in many languages (e.g. the Ethiopian languages or some of those of North America) the mountain does not have a 'foot'. Moreover, in English *eye* is used with a variety of other meanings, e.g. the centre of a hurricane or a spring of water, which are not so obviously related semantically to the organ of sight, yet it is not used for the centre of a flower or an indentation, though these might seem intuitively to be reasonable candidates for the extension of the meaning.

There are some other kinds of 'transference' that are more regular. Thus many adjectives may be used either literally for the quality referred to or with the transferred meaning of being the source of the quality. Thus a person may be *sad* and a book may be *sad*, while a coat may be *warm* in the two senses (either that it is of a certain degree of temperature or that it keeps one warm). The language recognises the difference of meaning in that we cannot say *John is as sad as the book he was reading*. This is similar to the traditional grammarian's concept of ZEUGMA (*She was wearing a white dress and a smile on her face*), for in each case one word co-occurs with two other words and these two each require the first to have a different meaning, and this the language does not allow. Similarly, many nouns have a concrete and an abstract sense. Thus we may compare *The score of the symphony is on the table* and *The score of the symphony is difficult to follow*. Notice once again that we cannot say *The score is on the table and difficult to follow*. Similar contrasts hold for *thesis, book, bible*, etc.

However, it is not always easy to decide whether a relationship is regular or not. English has intransitive and transitive (in the grammatical not the logical sense) uses of verbs such as *open* and *ring* – *The door opened, I opened the door, The bell rang, I rang the bell* (see 6.4). Slightly different are the basic and causative forms of *march, walk, run* – *He marched/ walked/ran a mile* vs. *He marched them up to the top of the hill, He walked the dog, He ran the children to school*. Now it would seem reasonable NOT to recognise homonymous pairs here and not, therefore, to say that there are two verbs *open*, two verbs *march*, etc. Yet the meaning relations are not wholly regular: does *walk the dog* mean 'cause the dog to walk'? Certainly *run the children* does not mean 'cause the children to run'. Moreover, not all verbs function in a similar way. We have no intransitive **The man wounded* and no causative **He swam them across the river*. An even less regular relationship is that found with *taste*, *feel* and *smell*, which may mean either 'have the sensation' or 'act to acquire the sensation' as in *I tasted salt in the porridge* and *I tasted the porridge*. But for the senses of sight and hearing we have different verbs to express these related meanings – *see* and *look at*, *hear* and *listen to*. Do we then decide that there are two verbs *taste*?

A third, and rather different way of attempting to establish polysemy rather than homonymy is to look for a central meaning or a core of meaning. This is possible where we have examples of metaphor or of the 'transferred' meanings we noted for *sad* and *score*. But in general it is very difficult to decide whether there is any central or core meaning. It is obvious enough why *key* is used not only for key of the door, but also for a translation or a keystone (one 'unlocks', the other 'locks'), but it is by no means easy to see why it is used for the keys of a piano and, therefore, not at all clear that this is an example of polysemy. Nor is there any obvious relation between *air* 'atmosphere' and the meanings of 'manner' and 'tune'. With verbs the problem is often even greater. *Charge* is used of electricity, of charging expenses, of a cavalry attack and of an accusation. These are quite far apart in their meanings. Can we discover a central or core meaning?

If we look at what has happened in history we see why the problem has arisen. Words change their meaning in quite surprising ways. Thus *arrive* is derived from Latin *ripa* 'a shore', and originally meant 'reach shore', while *rival* comes from Latin *rivus* 'a stream', rivals originally being people who shared the same stream. With such changes it is not surprising that meanings of *charge* should have so diverged – its earlier meaning is 'load', and it is related to *car* and even, in a less direct fashion, to *cargo*.

Fourthly, we can, perhaps, use the test of ambiguity. *I went to the bank* seems to be clearly ambiguous, since *bank* can mean either river bank or the place that deals with money. But decisions are not always easy. *Kill* is used to refer either to murdering or killing accidentally. The commandment *Thou shalt not kill* is to be understood in the first sense,

but *The motorist killed the child* in the second. Yet we should
not wish to say that *John killed Bill* is ambiguous. Slightly
more difficult is *I heard the girl crying*. Here it is far less clear
whether the two senses of *cry* ('weep' and 'shout') make us
conclude that there is ambiguity. Indeed, we shall be back
with precisely the kind of problem with which we started this
section – that of deciding whether there is or is not a difference of meaning.

It has been suggested that one test of ambiguity is the
'co-ordination test'. The sentence *John and Bill went to the
bank* cannot, it is argued, be taken to mean that one went to
the river and the other to the financial institution. Similarly,
The room and the furniture were light cannot be taken to mean
that the room was bright and the furniture not heavy. A
particular version of this is the 'do so' test – the fact that we
should not say *John went to the bank and so did Bill* with the
two meanings of *bank*. But these tests do not help, for
judgments about co-ordination depend upon judgments
about sameness of meaning, and the doubtful cases remain.
If we judge that *Mary cried and so did Ruth* is acceptable in
the sense that Mary wept and Ruth shouted, it will be because
we do not regard *cry* as ambiguous. In any case, the co-
ordination test will force us to make too many distinctions.
There is something curious about *John likes brunettes and
marshmallows* and *I saw Helen and a football match this after-
noon*, but these would hardly lead us to say that there are two
verbs *like* and two verbs *see*. As we have already seen, too, we
cannot say *The score is on the table and difficult to follow*; yet
this would (wrongly) suggest two distinct lexemes *score*.

It is not even the case that ambiguity itself is sufficient to
establish homonymy. Kempson (1977: 81) considers *He ran
the race for Hampshire*, which may mean either that he was a
competitor or that he organised the race. But since the two
meanings of *run* here are related in terms of causativity like
those of *walk* and *march*, it would be curious to suggest that
we have two lexical items. Ambiguity can result from grammatical as well as lexical differences. Thus, *They hit the ball* is

ambiguous between present and past tense, while *Flying planes can be dangerous* (Chomsky 1965: 21) is ambiguous because *flying planes* has two possible grammatical structures (with the meanings 'the act of flying planes' and 'planes that are flying'). The two meanings of *run* are of a semi-grammatical kind, *run* being in one case intransitive (though taking a so-called 'internal object' like *race*) and in the other transitive. Nothing is gained by treating these two uses of *run* as different lexical items, and no dictionary-maker would wish to do so.

However, a word that is polysemic will, naturally, have a variety of synonyms each corresponding to one of its meanings. It will often also have a set of antonyms. Thus *fair* may be used with (1) *hair*, (2) *skin*, (3) *weather*, (4) *sky*, (5) *judgment*, (6) *tackle*. The obvious antonyms would seem to be (1) *dark*, (2) *dark*, (3) *foul*, (4) *cloudy*, (5) *unfair*, (6) *foul*. (It is also used with *work* or *performance*, but there it is a middle term, 'neither good nor bad' and has, thus, no antonym.) It can be seen that *fair* with *hair* and *fair* with *skin* have the same antonym (*dark*), and so do *fair* with *weather* and *fair* with *tackle* (*foul*). We might be tempted to say that where the antonym is the same we have polysemy, and that difference of antonym implies homonymy. But this will suggest that *fair* with *weather* is more like *fair* with *tackle* than *fair* with *sky*. Intuitively, *sky* is more closely related to *weather* and *tackle* to *judgment*, but the antonyms do not provide evidence for this.

There may, in a few cases, be formal reasons for recognising homonymy. The French word *poli* means polished either in the literal or the transferred sense. This would seem to be a clear example of polysemy, but in the literal sense the word is linked with *dépolir* ('take polish off') and *polissage* ('polishing'), while in the other sense it goes with *impoli* ('unpolished' or 'impolite') and *politesse* ('politeness'). This seems to suggest that there are two different words that belong to two different related sets.

Notice, finally, that multiplicity of meaning is not confined to the words of the dictionary. It is also found with grammatical elements – the English past tense has two different meanings (3.1). So do some prefixes; *in-* usually means 'not', but this is not so in *inflammable*. (This word has led, through misunderstanding resulting from the ambiguity of the prefix, to some unfortunate accidents, and on the advice of Whorf it has become the practice in the USA to use the invented word *flammable* instead.) There is, as we have seen, similar ambiguity in syntax. Familiar examples are *The old men and women* and *Visiting relatives can be a nuisance*. Both can be analysed differently in syntax with accompanying difference of meaning. Multiplicity of meaning is a very general characteristic of language.

5.7 *Components*

In the previous sections we considered various sense relations without generally trying to relate them except by using the simplified logical formulae. A very different approach, it might seem at first sight, is analysis in terms of COMPONENTS – the total meaning of a word being seen in terms of a number of distinct elements or components of meaning. The notion of component does not introduce a further kind of relation; rather it purports to offer a theoretical framework for handling all the relations we have been discussing.

The idea that semantics could be handled in terms of components has been argued with the investigation of kinship terms. It was noted that in Spanish, for instance, the sex of the people involved is clearly marked – ending *-o* for male, *-a* for female as in (Lounsbury 1956: 158):

tio	'uncle'	*tia*	'aunt'
hijo	'son'	*hija*	'daughter'
abuelo	'grandfather'	*abuela*	'grandmother'
hermano	'brother'	*hermana*	'sister'

English has no markers of sex, of course, though the ending *-ess* occurs in *baroness*, *tigress*, *lioness*, *duchess*, etc. But if we are concerned with semantics that is not particularly relevant. There is no reason why we should not attempt to classify the English kinship terms with reference to categories such as sex, even if the language does not mark these terms in the form of the words.

Sex therefore provides one set of components for kinship terms; generation differences and degrees of relationship provide two others. Thus for generation differences we need at least five generations which may be labelled g_1, g_2, g_3, g_4, g_5. Then *grandfather* is g_1, *father*, *uncle*, etc., g_2, *brother*, *cousin*, g_3, *son*, *niece* g_4, and *grandson* g_5. On such a system the 'ego' (the person for whom the relationships hold) is, obviously g_3. Of course we would need others to deal with *great grandfather*, etc. Degrees of relationship involve LINEALITY – DIRECT for *grandfather*, *father*, COLINEAL for *brother*, *uncle* (but with different generation) and ABLINEAL for *cousin*. Given these three sets of components all the English kinship terms can be handled. *Aunt* is thus female, g_2 and colineal, *cousin* male or female, g_3 and ablineal. However, although this kind of approach to kinship has been important in the history of components, there are considerable doubts about its own 'reality' and about its relevance to the systems actually found in language (see 5.8).

We can most easily recognise components where words can be set out in a diagrammatic form to represent some kind of 'proportional' relationship. In English (and the same is true of many other languages) there is a three-fold division with many words that refer to living creatures:

man	*woman*	*child*
bull	*cow*	*calf*
ram	*ewe*	*lamb*
boar	*sow*	*piglet*

Thus *bull* is to *cow* as *ram* is to *ewe* – or in mathematical terms *bull* : *cow* : : *ram* : *ewe*. In the light of relationships such as these we can abstract the components (male) and (female), (adult) and (non-adult), plus (human), (bovine), (ovine) and (porcine). Strictly these examples do not distinguish (male) and (female) in full conjunction with (adult) and (non-adult),

since that would imply four possibilities and we only have
three. But all four are to be found in:

> *man   woman   boy   girl*

However, even with the other examples, it is more plausible
to make both distinctions than to say that there are simply
three possibilities – (male), (female) and (non-adult).

Analysis of this kind (COMPONENTIAL ANALYSIS) allows us
to provide definitions for all these words in terms of a few
components. Thus *boar* is (porcine), (male), (adult) and so
on. There are, as we saw earlier, gaps in the system – there
are no terms to distinguish between the male, female and the
young with giraffes or rhinoceroses. Often the distinction is
made by using a term taken from another set in conjunction
with the generic one – *bull elephant, cow elephant* and *elephant
calf*. Badgers are similarly *boars* and *sows* (though the young
are presumably *cubs*); the male fox is a *dog* or *dog-fox*, but the
female has a specific term *vixen*.

In many cases there is an appropriate word in the language
to label the component. *Male* and *female* are obvious examples. But it would be a mistake to suppose that if we use
such terms to define a common word that the resultant phrase
is semantically identical with it. Thus *boar* is not the same as
male adult porcine animal (see 5.3); it is important to note that
in the vocabulary of English we have words such as *boar*
and *bull*, whereas with *giraffe* we can only use the phrase
adult male giraffe; the difference is relevant to the semantic
structure of English.

Such labels are not, however, always readily available. We
have noted the semantic relationship (3.5):

> *come   go*
> *bring   take*

We noted that *come* is to *go* as *bring* is to *take* and we could
therefore distinguish components X and Y and A and B such
that *come* is XA and *go* XB, *bring* YA and *take* YB. But what
could be the names of the components? It is difficult to

provide an answer, for they cannot be identified with features that have any simple kind of physical reality. We may, perhaps, assume that all societies distinguish between male and female and that thus (male) and (female) are universal components of language. But the *come*, *go*, *bring*, *take* examples show that not all components are related to simple physical features such as sex, and it becomes less plausible to assume that they are universal (see 5.8).

A particular characteristic of componential analysis is that it attempts as far as possible to treat components in terms of 'binary' opposites, e.g. between (male) and (female), (animate) and (inanimate), (adult) and (non-adult). In this it clearly gives emphasis to the relation of complementarity (5.4). Notationally there is an advantage in such binary terms in that we can choose one only as the label and distinguish this in terms of plusses and minuses. Thus (male) and (female) are written as (+male) and (−male) and so on. We can, moreover, refer to the lack of a sex distinction as 'plus or minus' with the symbol (±male). But this works well only where there is a clear distinction; often there is indeterminacy, as with *tar* and *porridge* in relation to (solid)/(liquid).

In practice componential analysis has not been used simply in order to restate the relations discussed in earlier sections. Rather it has been used to bring out the logical relations that are associated with them. Thus by marking *man* as (+male) and *pregnant* as (−male), we can rule out **pregnant man*. Similarly by marking *boy* as (+male) (−adult) (+human) and *child* as (−adult) and (+human), we can establish that *There were two boys* entails *There were two children* and *Children are a nuisance* entails *Boys are a nuisance* (though the rules of entailment are obviously fairly complex).

Yet componential analysis does not handle all semantic relations well. First, it is difficult to reduce the relational opposites to components. For the relation of *parent/child* cannot simply be handled by assigning components to each, unless those components are in some sense directional. We could, that is to say, treat these as having the same components, but in a different 'direction'; but by introducing 'direction' into components we are, in effect, admitting that they ARE relational and not simply 'atomic' components of meaning. Secondly, the componential analysis cannot remove the hierarchical characteristic of hyponymy. For the distinction (+male)/(−male) applies only to living (animate) things. Distinction in terms of these components, e.g. between *ram* and *ewe*, will hold only for items that are also marked as (+animate). In a straight hierarchical diagram this is easily shown, and is a natural consequence of the hierarchy. In a componential analysis it still has to be stated, for it is necessary to rule out not only *pregnant ram* but also *pregnant table*; the point here is that the component (−male) is restricted to those items which have (+animate). Componential analysis therefore has to state that, only if something is animate, may it be male or female with a formula such as (+animate ±male). Again it will be obvious that such rules (called 'redundancy rules') are simply a disguised way of stating the hierarchical nature of the semantic distinctions. Componential analysis can thus handle all the relations we have discussed, simply because it can be made to do so, with the relevant modifications. But it is doubtful whether it makes them clearer; it seems rather to obscure their differences.

The componential approach to semantics is basic to Katz & Fodor's 'The structure of a semantic theory' (1963). This work has been of such interest that it deserves some consideration here and, although Katz (1966: 151–75) modified his views, I shall use it as the basis of the discussion. As we have already seen (2.3), Katz & Fodor are concerned essentially with ambiguity, anomaly and paraphrase. The arguments are, however, very largely based upon ambiguity – upon showing that a sentence may have two readings. Thus *The bill is large* is ambiguous until it is disambiguated by . . . *but need not be paid*.

Turning to the structure of vocabulary, they point out that a dictionary would distinguish between four meanings of the word *bachelor* – (1) a man who has never married, (2) a young knight serving under the banner of another, (3) someone with a first degree, (4) a young male unmated fur seal during the mating season. These four meanings can, moreover, be partly differentiated by what they call 'markers' which are shown in round brackets, e.g. (human) (animal) and (male), together with some specific characteristics which are called 'distinguishers' and placed in square brackets, e.g. [first degree] in the case of the academic. The semantics of *bachelor* can thus be set out in a tree diagram (Figure 6). An important question, however, is 'How do we establish which precisely are the markers?' The answer that is given is that they are those features that allow us to disambiguate a sentence. An illustration provided by the authors is *The old bachelor finally died*. This cannot refer to the fur seal, because such bachelors are by definition young. It follows from this that (young) must be a marker for the fur seal, and that it must now appear not among the distinguishers as in Figure 6, but as a marker.

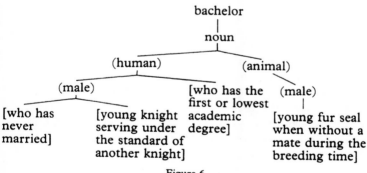

Figure 6

The theory has one major drawback. There is, in theory, no limit to the number of markers that can be established. For (as we saw earlier in 3.2) any piece of information can be used to disambiguate and can thus function as a marker. For instance, *The bachelor wagged his flippers* is hardly ambiguous – it must refer to the fur seal. *The bachelor got his hair wet*, on the other hand, cannot refer to the fur seal, though it might refer to any of the other three. If we use the disambiguation test we have, for the fur seal, the markers (having flippers) and (not having hair) – and the list is endless. Katz (1966: 154–5) dropped the distinction between marker and distinguisher, but the difficulty remains. However we tackle the problem, we shall be faced with an infinite set of components, because in principle ANY piece of information may be used to disambiguate a sentence.

5.8 *The problem of universals*

We have already noted several times that there is a question about the universality of semantic features – whether they or some of them at least occur (and even must occur) in all languages. At one extreme there is the Sapir–Whorf hypothesis (3.1), which suggests that each language may 'create' its own world and so its own semantics. At the other it could be argued that such components as (male) and (female) are found in all languages and that there are many others too, e.g. the basic colours (4.3) and kinship relations (5.7).

The simplest form of the universalist view is that there is a universal inventory of semantic features (components). But what is the relation between this inventory and the set of features found in individual languages? The strongest claim would be that all languages make use of the whole inventory and so have the same features. A weaker claim is that each language uses only SOME of the features in the total inventory. The first answer seems highly implausible in view of what seem to be very obvious differences in languages; it can only be made to work by arguing that all the semantic features can be exhibited somehow in each language, though some will be more central. (This is tantamount to saying that if something can be said in one language, it can be said in another.) The second answer might seem more plausible – all languages have 'male', 'female', 'black', 'white', etc., but many other features are found only in some languages. But neither this view nor the stronger view makes a verifiable claim unless a finite inventory of features is produced. For let us suppose that we discover a language which appears to have features that have never been noted before. If we simply add them to the inventory, the claim about the universality of the inventory becomes quite trivial. The claim cannot be disproved, even in principle, if every counter-example can be dealt with in this way.

A still weaker claim is that only some features are universal, while the rest are characteristic of individual languages. This may well be true, though it may not even be that the 'universal' features are exactly the same in each language. This seems to be the case with the colour terms and categories. We do not find identity, but only close similarity.

Let us, however, accept the weakest universalist claim – that languages share some semantic features. What kind of explanation can we give? There are at least five answers:

(1) 'The world is like that.'
(2) The structure of the minds of all people is basically the same.
(3) The cultural needs of different societies are similar.
(4) There is or has been contact between different societies with different languages.
(5) The languages of the world all have a common origin.

There may be some truth in all of these answers, and it is not at all easy to separate them.

The first two replies (in terms of the world and mind) raise the philosophical problem of objective and subjective reality. Is our experience like it is because that is what the world is like, or because that is how our minds interpret it? Nevertheless, we can sometimes distinguish between what would seem to be physical reality and psychological reality. The sex distinctions in 'male'/'female' have an objective, physical basis, as do the differences indicated by *cow*, *horse*, *elephant*, etc., whereas if it is true that different people make (roughly) the same colour distinctions, these do not 'exist' in physical terms but are part of the psychology of perception (and the same is certainly true of our perception of speech sounds).

It is very important to recognise that the fact that there is some kind of physical reality does not necessarily make it the basis of a semantic analysis. A good example of this is kinship terminology. Since most societies have fairly strict rules of 'kindred and affinity' (as the Book of Common Prayer calls them), kinship relations can usually be stated wholly in terms of a family tree which depends on the parent–child and the husband–wife relationships. But there are two objections to the type of componential analysis suggested in 5.7. First, there are alternative, equally plausible, analyses of the same relationships. Secondly, and more importantly, in some languages the linguistic system bears very little resemblance to any of these analyses. Thus in Pawnee the term that we might translate as 'father' is used of all the males whose relationship is traceable through the father, while 'uncle' is used of the males traceable through the mother, and conversely, all the females traceable through the mother are 'mother' and all the females traceable through the father are 'aunt'. The rules for 'son', 'daughter', 'nephew', 'niece' are the converse of these (Lounsbury 1956).

We must not, of course, ignore the influence of cultures upon the linguistic systems, and it is likely that kinship terminology, for example, will be much more a reflection of them than of the actual objective relationships. But it will not always be easy, or even possible, to distinguish between cultural reality and physical or psychological reality.

In the case of colour terminology, too, there may be three factors at work. First, there are some objective features – the green of living plants, the red of blood, the blue of the sky. Secondly, it may be that there is some psychological reality to the foci. Thirdly, cultural considerations may make certain colour distinctions important, as was shown for Navaho (4.3).

Finally, it may be that some apparent universals are no more than an accident of the history of languages in either of the two ways indicated by the last two replies. It would appear that the modern Welsh system of colour is now much more like that of English, as a result of increasing bilingualism. We cannot be sure how far similar contacts have brought other linguistic systems closer. Certainly it is the case that in most semantic areas (and certainly in colour systems) the languages of Europe have much in common. Nor can we be sure about the historical relationship of languages. For the language families for which we have evidence, we can go back only a few thousand years, and it could be that all the extant languages of the world have a common ancestor (and that need not make any assumptions about the origin of language itself). If so, some, at least, of the universal-like features of language may simply be accidental in the sense that our languages could also have developed in quite different ways and from quite different origins.

6

SEMANTICS AND GRAMMAR

Grammar and semantics are often thought of as separate levels of linguistics. Nevertheless, it is clear that grammatical categories often have meaning, that we must have a place for sentence meaning (see 2.5) and that the sentence is essentially a grammatical unit.

6.1 *Formal grammar*

Most of the traditional grammarians assumed that grammatical categories were essentially semantic. Nouns were defined as names of things, gender was concerned with sex, while plural simply meant 'more than one'.

On the other hand, many linguists have argued that grammar must be kept distinct from semantics and that grammatical categories must be wholly defined in terms of the FORM of the language, the actually observable features. (It is unfortunate that the term *form* is also used for *form* words as opposed to *full* words. This is a completely different and much more restricted use of the term and must not be confused with its use here.) One of the earliest statements is in Sapir (1921: 33, 59ff.), but Sapir, it will be remembered, believed in linguistic relativity (3.1), and his point was essentially that, since each language had a different formal structure, it presented a different world. Bloomfield (1933: 140) took a similar line for a different reason (3.4) – that we must be 'scientific' and that the study of meaning was a weak point in linguistic theory. He insisted, therefore, that formal features, not meaning, should be the starting point of a linguistic discussion.

There are two good arguments for excluding meaning

from grammar, i.e. in favour of FORMAL GRAMMAR. The first is that meaning is often very vague and meaning categories are not easily delineated. Moreover, because of this vagueness, what might seem to be obvious semantic categories are often in fact definable only in terms of the formal features of a language (to this extent Whorf may have been right). If, then, the grammatical categories are given semantic definitions, the definitions are circular. An excellent example is the definition so often found in grammar books of a noun as 'a word used for naming anything'. The difficulty is that we have no way of establishing what 'anything' may be. To be of any value the definition must establish independently of the language what are 'the things' that may be named. We find that in English such things include fire, speed, place, intelligence, suffering, as well as objects such as tables and chairs. Moreover, they include redness and blackness, but not 'red' and 'black'. What reason have we for believing that these are all 'things' and how, in particular, do we know that *redness* and *blackness* are names of 'things', while *red* and *black* are not? Similarly, why does *rain* refer to a 'thing', while *It's raining* does not? It is reported that there are some languages in which words for 'river', 'spring', etc., are essentially verbs so that a literal translation would be 'It's rivering' rather than 'There's a river' (see 3.1). How, then, do we recognise 'things'? The answer is painfully simple -- 'things' are what are designated by nouns. The definition of the noun in terms of 'naming anything' is thus completely circular; the circularity arises because we have no non-linguistic way of defining 'things'.

A second argument for formal grammar is that, even when we can establish semantic and grammatical categories independently, they often do not coincide. One of the best known examples is that of *wheat* and *oats*, where there is a clear lack of correspondence between grammatical number, singular and plural, with numerical quantity. That these are singular and plural respectively is shown not so much by the -*s* ending of *oats* as by the agreement with the verb -- *The wheat is in the barn, The oats are in the barn.* Yet in terms of 'one' and 'more than one' *wheat* and *oats* cannot be distinguished. No one, surely, would seriously argue that *wheat* is a single mass, while *oats* consist of a collection of individual grains. There are many other similar examples. *Hair* is singular in English, but French and Italian have a plural noun, *cheveux*, *capelli*; it is not to be supposed that there is any difference in the way we look at hair. Similarly gender and sex are distinct in German and French. The German words for 'young woman' are neuter, *Mädchen* and *Fräulein*, while the feminine *la sentinelle* in French may refer to a strapping young male. In English tense is not directly related to time since the past tense is used for future time in e.g. *If he came tomorrow* . . . (see 3.1). It is clear from such examples that the basic grammatical categories of a language must be established independently of their meaning. It is not surprising that different languages have different grammatical systems.

Nevertheless, once we have established the formal categories, we can proceed to discuss their meaning. We shall then find that there is some correlation between e.g. gender and sex, tense and time, grammatical number and enumeration, though the correlation will never be exact. Thus in French the nouns referring specifically to females are always feminine, even though feminine nouns may refer to males, and in English ONE of the functions of tense is to refer to time. Indeed it is only because there is some correlation that the labels 'gender', 'tense', etc., have any usefulness at all; the danger is that we should think that such labels are semantic definitions.

It is, however, as so often in semantics, a mistake to draw a very clear distinguishing line. As we go into more detailed investigation of grammar, we find the correlation between grammar and semantics becomes closer and closer, until we reach a stage where it is difficult, if not impossible, to declare whether the categories are formal or semantic. For consider **John is seeming happy.* We could say this is ungrammatical on the grounds that the verb *seem* does not occur in the progressive (continuous) form *is seeming*. But is this in fact a grammatical rule or is it the case that for semantic reasons John cannot be in a continuous state of seeming? There is no clear answer – the line between grammar and semantics is not a clear one. Similarly, let us compare **John is having gone there* and **John continued having gone there*. There is little doubt that the first is ruled out grammatically by a simple rule that puts auxiliary *have* before auxiliary *be* and so allows only *John has been going there*. But it is not clear whether we ought to say that there is a grammatical rule that prevents *continue* from being followed by a form of auxiliary *have*, or whether we should say that it makes little sense semantically.

We find, then, that there are two rather puzzling aspects of the relation between grammar and meaning. First, although we can, and must, set up formal categories, they will be found to have some correlation, but not one-to-one, with semantics. Secondly, we find that there is a difficult borderline area. There is a third point – that some of the major categories seem to be found in all languages. As far as we know, there is no language that does not distinguish in some way between nouns and verbs, even though some may not have different word-classes (parts of speech). The similarities between languages support some kind of universalist view, even if only a weak one. It is also not surprising if some of the more important semantic categories, e.g. those relating to sex, quantity, time, are found to be represented in many grammatical systems. But grammar is learnt by succeeding generations and is thus to some degree a matter of convention. This accounts for the 'oddity' of *oats* and *wheat* and of the 'female' neuter nouns in German.

The controversy about semantics and formal grammar was revived a few years ago in terms of 'interpretive' and 'generative' semantics within transformational-generative grammar. Chomsky (1965: 16ff.) had argued that there is a syntactic DEEP STRUCTURE and that it is at this level that we can relate active and passive sentences, and, indeed, that the only difference between an active and its related passive sentence would be the absence or presence of an element *Passive*. Thus *John played the piano* is to be analysed in terms of *John*, *play*, *past tense*, *the piano* while *The piano was played by John* is to be analysed in terms of *John*, *play*, *past tense*, *the piano* and *Passive*. (This is a grossly oversimplified account, but illustrates the points that are relevant here.) Similarly, we can relate the statement *John is coming* and the question *Is John coming?* in terms of the presence or absence of *Q* (*Question*). The difference in the order of the words (as well as other differences) in the paired sentences is a matter of their SURFACE STRUCTURE.

In these examples the surface structures are very different, but the deep structures are similar and differ only in the presence or absence of a single element. There are other pairs of sentences with similar surface structures but quite different deep structures. One well-known pair is *John is eager to please* and *John is easy to please*. The deep structures will have to indicate that *John* is the 'deep' subject of *please* in the first and the object of *please* in the second, and also that while *John* is the subject of *is* in the first, the subject of *is* is '— please John' in the second. Very roughly, we need deep structures to suggest *John is eager* (*John please* —) and (— *please John*) *is easy* (the blanks indicating unstated subjects and objects).

Part of the syntax is concerned with rules (transformational rules) that convert deep structures into surface structures. It is essential that given the deep structure these rules will automatically generate the correct surface structure. The deep structures are generated by the BASE which consists of two components – the CATEGORIAL COMPONENT and the LEXICON. The former contains the whole of the grammatical apparatus and the latter the inventory of all the lexical items. Thus the deep structures will contain all the necessary grammatical and all the necessary lexical information. Thus to return to our first pair of examples, we need to take into account the presence of the lexical items *John*, *play*, *piano*, but also the grammatical status of *John* and *the piano* as noun phrases and *play* as a verb (for without this we might generate such non-sentences as **The piano is Johnned by play*). The first set of information is provided by the lexicon, the second by the categorial component of the base.

The information contained in the deep structures will allow us to do two things. First, we can generate the surface structures. Thus the presence of *Passive* will ensure that *The piano* is placed in initial position and *John* is placed after *by*. Secondly, we can arrive at the semantics from the deep structure by rules of semantic interpretation. Given, that is to say, the grammatical and lexical information that the deep structure of a sentence provides, we can in theory say what that sentence means. It is in this sense that Chomsky's model is 'interpretive'.

Other scholars argued that, if there is a deep structure, it must be much deeper, so deep, in fact, that it is essentially semantic and not syntactic. In that sense the semantics is not interpretive; since it is the actual source of the syntax, it is 'generative'. The arguments are many and complex. One of the most striking is that the deep structure analysis of the active/passive relationship seems to break down with *Many men read few books* and *Few books are read by many men*. For these are clearly different in meaning. The first says that lots of men read very little, but the second that there are few books (e.g. the Bible, Shakespeare) that are read by a lot of people. There is a similar difference between *Many arrows didn't hit the target* and *The target wasn't hit by many arrows*. To analyse such pairs of sentences as having the same deep structure, except for the presence of the passive marker, is clearly most unsatisfactory. The deep structures, it is argued (Lakoff 1971a: 238–45), must be the semantic structures, which, in effect, say, 'The men who read few books are many' and 'The books that many men read are few'. A rather different argument (Lakoff 1968) suggested that *Seymour sliced the salami with a knife* should be related to *Seymour used a knife to slice the salami*, and that they have essentially the same deep structure. (Fillmore's case theory (6.7) is also within generative semantics.)

The controversy is now largely dead, because both sides have abandoned their positions, though Chomsky still maintains that syntax is AUTONOMOUS, i.e. independent of semantics (cf. Chomsky 1977: 36–9). But generative semantics was almost certainly doomed to failure, because of the impossibility of using semantics as a basis for grammar. The arguments in favour of formal grammar ought to have served as a warning.

6.2 *Grammatical categories*

Let us now look briefly at some familiar grammatical categories – gender, number and person.

We shall not expect to find an exact correlation between gender and sex. Indeed sometimes we have a surprising contrast as in the French for 'the male mouse' which is *la souris mâle* ('the (feminine) male mouse'), for *souris* is a feminine noun. Similarly we noted *Mädchen* and *Fräulein* and *la sentinelle* in the previous section. Yet although in some cases the gender is wholly idiosyncratic, we can at other times see some regularity. The German words are neuter because all words with the diminutive ending *-chen* and *-lein* are neuter, while in French occupational names such as *sentinelle* are all feminine. The explanation then lies in historical facts, which have overruled the obvious semantic probability that male creatures will be referred to by masculine nouns and female creatures by feminine ones.

There is no real problem in English, for English has, strictly, no grammatical gender at all. It has, of course, the pronouns *he*, *she* and *it*, but these are essentially markers of sex. The first two, *he* and *she*, are used if the sex is specifically indicated or known; otherwise *it* is used. There is, however, one qualification. There is a difference between the use of the pronouns for animals and for humans. *It* may be used for animals, e.g. to refer to a dog, and so may *he* or *she* if the sex is known. However, with humans *it* cannot be used, even if the sex is unknown. For the indefinite unknown human the forms *they*, *them*, *their* are used in colloquial English (even for singular) as in *Has anyone lost their hat? If anyone comes tell them to go away*. This is frowned on by some grammarians, but seems to me to be a useful and wholly acceptable device for avoiding the indication of sex. For reference to a specific human whose sex is unknown, e.g. a baby, *it* is sometimes used, but it is probably wiser to ask the mother first 'Is it a boy or a girl?'

Many languages have noun classes that function grammatically like the gender classes of the Indo-European and Semitic languages. Thus, in Swahili, there are classes of animates, of small things and of big things, each class clearly indicated formally by an appropriate prefix and requiring agreement with adjectives and verbs. These are often referred to as 'gender classes'. If we are thinking primarily of the grammatical function, that they are classes of nouns that require agreement with adjectives and verbs, the term 'gender' is appropriate, since that is essentially the grammatical function of gender in the more familiar languages. But, of course, it may be argued that some other term that does not suggest a relation with sex should be found (though the purist might be reminded that etymologically *gender* is not related to sex, but merely means 'kind'). Even with noun classes of the type that are not related to sex we find that there is no precise correspondence between formal class and its meaning. Not all the nouns of the 'small things' class in Swahili are small, while Bloomfield (1933: 272) relates that in the Algonquian languages of North America there is a grammatical distinction between animate and inanimate nouns, but that both 'kettle' and 'raspberry' belong to the class of animates, though 'strawberry' is inanimate.

We have similarly noted anomalies with number. Semantically, the question of enumeration does not seem to be a very important one. Many languages have grammatical number systems, but others in various parts of the world (e.g. South-East Asia, West Africa) do not. Moreover, it is difficult to see why SEMANTICALLY the essential distinction should be between singular ('one') and plural ('more than one'). Many languages make this distinction in their grammar, but not all. Some classical languages – Sanskrit, Greek and Arabic – had, in addition, dual – referring to two objects. Other languages, e.g. Fijian and Tigre (Ethiopia), have distinctions of 'little plurals' and 'big plurals' too. If we look at the problem of counting objectively it is not at all obvious that there are any 'natural' numerical classes that might be expected to be shown in the grammar of all or most languages.

More important, perhaps, is the need to distinguish between individual and mass. This is a distinction that English makes quite clearly, though it is often ignored in the grammar books. The category is referred to as COUNTABILITY, with the noun classes of COUNTABLES and UNCOUNTABLES or COUNT and MASS. Examples of count nouns are *cat* and *book*, while *butter* and *petrol* are mass nouns. Formally the two classes are easily distinguished. Count nouns alone may occur in the singular with the indefinite article *a* – *a cat* (but not **a butter*), while only mass nouns may occur with no article or with the indefinite quantifier *some* (not *some* in the sense of 'some or other') – *Butter is . . .*, *some butter* (but not **Cat is . . .*, **some cat*). Some nouns, e.g. *cake, fish*, belong to both classes.

The semantic difference between these two classes is clear enough. The count nouns 'individuate' – they indicate individual specimens, while the mass nouns refer to a quantity that is not individuated in this way. But the distinction does not correspond closely to any semantic distinction in the world of experience, and this should be no cause for surprise. It is true that liquids are always referred to by mass nouns because they cannot be individuated. There is no obvious object that can be described as **a water*. But there is no explanation in semantic terms why *butter* is a mass noun while *jelly* is count as well as mass; there is no semantic reason why we can refer to a single mass of jelly as *a jelly* but not to a mass of butter as **a butter*. On the other hand, while *cake* is count as well as mass, for the obvious reason that individual cakes can be recognised, *bread* is only mass – we cannot talk of *a bread, but have to use a different word, *loaf*. A foreigner could not guess, then, whether such words as *soap*, *trifle*, *cheese* would be count nouns in English. He has, moreover, to learn the 'individuating' nouns *loaf of bread*, *cake of soap*, *pat of butter*.

The count/mass distinction is a fairly clear one – it classifies English nouns, though some belong to both classes. But mass nouns can, nevertheless, function as count nouns. Two obvious functions are, first, the use of such expressions as *a butter*, *a petrol* to mean 'a kind of butter' or 'a kind of petrol', and secondly *a coffee*, *a beer* to mean 'a cup of coffee' and 'a glass of beer'. It is best to treat these nouns as 'basically' mass nouns and these functions as types of individuation that can be applied to them for specific purposes – to indicate kinds and, with liquids, familiar quantities. Similarly, count nouns that refer to creatures may function as mass nouns to indicate the meat; we find not merely familiar usages such as *chicken*, *rabbit*, *fish* but can also freely form mass nouns *elephant*, *crocodile* and even *dog* (*The Chinese eat dog*) to refer to the meat. (But we have, of course, the specific words *beef*, *mutton*, *pork*, *venison* for the flesh of cattle, sheep, pigs and deer.)

Semantically, mass nouns are nearer to plurals than to singular forms of count nouns. This accounts for the anomaly of *oats* and *wheat* – there is little difference, unless it is clearly specified, between a large number of grains and a mass of them. In some languages liquids are not mass nouns, but plurals, e.g. in Bilin the word for 'water'.

The term 'count' is relevant to the fact that most count nouns can be counted – *one book, two/three/four books*. But there are two reservations. First, English has the words *scissors, trousers, shears, tongs*, etc., which are formally plural, but cannot be enumerated except by using another noun *a pair of* —; this is formally like the individuators of the mass nouns, *a cake of soap, a pat of butter*. Secondly, although English uses the plural form with numerals above one, not all languages do. In Welsh, for instance, 'four dogs' is *pedwar ci*, though 'dog' is *ci* and 'dogs' *cwn*. In Tigre there are many mass nouns which have a singulative (individuating) form made by a suffix, e.g. *nəhəb* 'bees', but *nəhbät* 'a bee'. But the singulative form is the form used with all numerals, not merely 'one' – *ḥätte nəhbät* 'one bee', *säläs nəhbät* 'three bees', etc. What seems to be important here is not plurality, but individuation.

The category of person (first person *I*, *we*, second person *you*, third person *he*, *she*, *it*, *they*) is often closely associated with number and with gender in the verbal forms of languages. (In Western Indo-European languages only number and person are marked in the verb, but in Semitic languages and Eastern Indo-European languages gender is also associated with it.) But, as we saw in 3.5, person is essentially a deictic category.

The precise function of any set of person markers, usually the pronouns, but also the endings of verbs in some languages, may vary from language to language, but all can basically be interpreted in terms of speaker, hearer, and those who are non-participants in the conversation or written correspondence, and this is the basis of first, second and third person.

There are some complications. First, languages have plural person markers, and it might be assumed that these refer simply to several speakers, several hearers and several non-participants. But this is not always so. It is rare for there to be several speakers, except in chorus as, for instance, a crowd at a football match crying *We want another* or an impatient group singing *Why are we waiting? We* usually refers not to a plurality of speakers ('I and I and . . .') but to speaker and hearer ('I and you'), speaker and non-participant ('I and he/she') or speaker, hearer and non-participant ('I and you and he/she'), plus any further combinations involving more than one speaker, hearer or non-participant. *You* may well refer to several hearers, but it may also be used to refer to hearer (or hearers) plus non-participant (or non-participants) ('you and he/she', etc.). *They* alone will always refer simply to a number of non-participants. There is in fact a simple rule with the plural: the pronoun is determined by the 'highest' ranking person included. If *I* is included, use *we*; if it is not but *you* is, use *you*; otherwise use *they*. But some languages make other distinctions. Not uncommon are distinct forms for inclusive plural 'I and you' and for exclusive plural 'I and he/she'. Secondly, as we saw in 3.5, in many languages person is involved in matters of politeness, and there are sometimes quite complex reasons for choosing the appropriate form.

There are other forms with deictic functions. We have already discussed some of these, but the articles are also of interest. The definite article *the* is used to refer to a single identifiable item in the context, where it is apparent to speaker and hearer precisely what that item is. Thus, although *book* may refer to any book, *the book* refers to a particular book that both speaker and hearer can identify, either one that is being talked about or one that is recognisable in the non-linguistic context, e.g. visible on the table before them. Identification of the item is often simply in terms of the most familiar. *The Government* will usually refer to our government, *the moon* to the moon that we see at night. Similarly *the kitchen* or *the garden* will refer to our own kitchen or garden, or, if we are in someone else's house, to theirs. But this can change – we may be talking about another government, the moon of another planet or the kitchen and garden of another house. What matters is that the item can be identified in the context without misunderstanding.

Because of its function the article does not normally occur with names (proper nouns). A proper noun such as *Fred*, *Professor Brown*, etc., is used simply to identify a particular person, and the article would thus be redundant (though it is used, redundantly, in some languages, e.g. Italian). However, even proper nouns are sometimes used in a non-unique sense; thus we can talk about *the three Freds* to mean three people with the name Fred. We can even refer to someone in one of their aspects, e.g. *He's not the Fred I knew*. In such cases we identify a particular Fred or kinds of Fred and the article may be used. There are, however, some idiosyncrasies about the use of the article. Thus rivers are identified with the article – *the Severn*, *the Thames*, etc., but cities are not – *London*, *Bristol*, etc. (except for *The Hague*). This is a purely formal grammatical point and has no semantic significance.

It is of some interest that if an item becomes uniquely identifiable the article is dropped. Thus we now have *Parliament*, not *the Parliament* and, more surprisingly, perhaps, *Bank rate* and not *the Bank rate*. Since there is only one of each, the noun phrase has, in effect, become a name, a proper noun.

6.3 *Grammar and lexicon*

We noted, in 2.4, the distinction made by Sweet in terms of full words and form words. Full words are essentially those that can be dealt with satisfactorily in the dictionary, while the form words (although always listed in dictionaries) have to be discussed in relation to the grammar of the language. For modern linguists the distinction is between LEXICON and grammar. Other scholars have made similar distinctions. An American linguist, Fries (1952: 65ff.), recognised only four 'parts of speech' but fifteen sets of 'function words'. The parts of speech were, in effect, noun, verb, adjective and adverb, though Fries quite deliberately refused to call them by these traditional names; examples from each of the sets of function words are *the*, *may*, *not*, *very*, *and*, *at*, *do*, *there*, *why*, *although*, *oh*, *yes*, *listen!*, *please*, *let's*.

Grammar, however, is not restricted to the study of form or function words. It is concerned, more widely, with categories such as tense, gender, number and with syntactic functions such as subject and object. Some of these may be marked in a language by form words, but they may equally be marked by morphemes (assuming we accept the suggestions in 2.4) or even by the order of the words. While there is a problem of establishing what are the relevant grammatical categories in any language, it is irrelevant for semantics whether a grammatical category is indicated by a form word, a morpheme or the order of the words. For example, we find that English marks past tense with the past tense morpheme (usually indicated as *-ed*). But there is no similar morpheme to indicate the future; this is marked by the verbs *shall* and *will* or by *be going to* (it may also be indicated by other verbal forms with the appropriate adverbs as in *I'm flying to Cairo tomorrow* and *I fly to Cairo tomorrow*). Other languages may use inflection where English and most familiar languages use form words. Thus the English conjunctions *after*, *when*, *while*, *if* are translated into Bilin (a Cushitic language of Ethiopia) by endings of the verb. Nearer home, Finnish has a very complex 'case' system, containing not only 'nominative', 'accusative', 'ablative' etc., all of which are familiar from Latin, but also 'elative', 'illative', 'adessive', 'essive' and others. These last ones would translate English *out of*, *into*, *on*, *as*.

In modern linguistics the problem of the distinction between the grammar and the lexicon is often posed in terms of the distinction between sentences that are unacceptable or 'deviant' for grammatical reasons, and those that are excluded on lexical grounds. There is no apparent difficulty about recognising a grammatically deviant sentence. An example would be **The boys is in the garden*. This breaks only one grammatical rule, but we can easily invent sentences that seem to conform to no rules at all as **Been a when I tomato*. In contrast we shall rule out on different grounds **The water is fragile*, **The flower walked away*. With these the issue is one of collocation (see 4.4), which determines the possible co-occurrence of lexical items and here rules out the co-occurrence of *water* with *fragile* and *flower* with *walk*.

There have, however, been opposing views on the question whether these two kinds of restriction, one grammatical, the other lexical, are, in principle, different. One argument to sustain the difference is that a sentence can be grammatically correct, yet at the same time totally deviant in lexical terms. Thus Chomsky invented the sentence *Colourless green ideas sleep furiously*, which seems impeccable grammatically, yet is lexically completely unacceptable. If a sentence can thus conform to grammar, but be completely deviant lexically, it would seem that grammar and lexicon are distinct. Earlier, incidentally, Carnap had made the same point by inventing a sentence that does not contain any English word at all yet seems to be quite grammatical in terms of English – *Pirots karulize elatically* (1937: 2).

Some linguists believed that just as grammar could be wholly formal, and that we need not concern ourselves with the meaning of any of our grammatical categories, so, too, a total statement of all the collocational possibilities of a word would be sufficient to characterise it linguistically. Indeed, some went so far as to believe that the set of collocational possibilities of a word was essentially the meaning of that word for the linguist (Joos 1950 [1958: 356]). It was in that spirit that synonymy was defined in terms of total interchangeability (see 5.3). This is, of course, to take one extreme view of the relation between semantics and collocation, one that makes collocation determine meaning (whereas the other extreme view sees meaning as totally determining collocation).

Rather surprisingly, perhaps, even Chomsky (1965: 95ff.) attempted to handle collocational possibilities within grammar. He advocated a grammar that, given a set of appropriate rules, would generate all and only the grammatical sentences of a language. What is relevant to semantics is that he was concerned with restrictions on the co-occurrence of items within a sentence, so that we shall not permit **The idea cut the tree*, **I drank the bread*, **He frightened that he was coming*, **He elapsed the man*. In all these examples it is clear that we have chosen items that, in some way, do not 'fit' the verbs. The last examples are clearly a matter of grammar in that *frighten* does not take a *that*-clause, while *elapse* is an intransitive verb that does not take any object at all. With the other two examples it is a matter, however, of the incompatibility of lexical items, of certain nouns (as subjects or objects) with certain verbs. While noting the difference between these two types, Chomsky proposed to deal with them in similar ways. In both cases he stated, as part of the specification of the verb, the environment in which it may occur. Thus *elapse* was shown as not occurring with an object noun phrase, and *frighten* not occurring with a following *that*-clause (or rather it was NOT shown that they can so occur, since the specification would state what is possible, not what is not possible). Similarly *cut* would be shown to need a 'concrete' subject, and *drink* a 'liquid' object. This was achieved in terms of components, by stating that the relevant subject and object must have the components (concrete) and (liquid). These are SELECTIONAL RESTRICTIONS. Any sentence which did not comply to them was ruled out and the grammar would not generate it.

Although this appears very neat it is quite unsatisfactory for a number of reasons. First, we have, once again, the problem of the limitless number of components required (see 5.7). For if we are to rule out all the anomalous sentences, we shall have to include all relevant information – and this is infinite. Secondly, the theory fails to account, without considerable complications, for the many occasions in which such selectional restrictions are legitimately broken. This is possible with verbs of saying, thinking, etc., as in *John thought we could drink bread*, or with some negatives, e.g. *You can't drink bread*. It is obvious that we are concerned here with 'making sense', and that is a matter of semantics rather than grammar. For we can be grammatical and still not make sense as Chomsky himself illustrated with his famous *Colourless green ideas sleep furiously* (1957: 15). But the important question is not whether it is possible to handle such restrictions as part of the grammar, but rather whether there is any justification at all for doing so. For we surely do not wish to say that **John drank the meat* is ungrammatical in the same sense as is **The boys is in the garden*. The difference seems clear enough to us as native speakers of the language, for, if we are confronted with deviant sentences of these two types, our reactions are different. If a grammatical rule is broken, we can, and usually will, correct the sentence, e.g. to *The boys are in the garden*, while if the sentence conforms to no grammatical rules we simply rule it out as gibberish. Where, however, the deviance lies in the collocational (selectional) restrictions, i.e. is lexical, we shall usually try to make sense of the sentence by looking for a context in which it might be used, for we would normally assume that collocations imply some semantic compatibility. For instance, *John drinks fish* might seem to be deviant, until we think about fish soup, and it is by no means difficult to find a poetic interpretation (or even possibly a scientific one) for *The water is fragile*. Even Chomsky's *Colourless green ideas sleep furiously* can be (and has been) given an interpretation, far fetched though it has to be.

The lexical restrictions, it has been suggested (Haas 1973: 147–8), are not a matter of rules but of tendencies, not of Yes/no, but of More/less, when judged in terms of deviance. Unfortunately this leads us to the problem 'When is a rule a rule?', for there is no clear line between grammatical and lexical deviance. Some sentences are clearly ungrammatical and are simply to be ruled out or corrected, while others are odd only in a lexical way and can, with some imagination, be contextualised. But there are others that are half-way, and we are not really sure whether their deviance is lexical or grammatical.

Consider, for example, *The dog scattered*. This is not simply a matter of the collocation of *dog* with *scatter*, for the verb *scatter* is normally used only with plural nouns (*The dogs scattered*), or with collective nouns (*The herd scattered*). It would seem, therefore, that a grammatical rule is being broken and that we should amend to *The dogs scattered* (or *The dog was scattered*). But cannot we imagine a dog with magical powers whose way of avoiding its enemies was to break into many pieces and 'scatter' over a wide area? Indeed we can, and so we have found a possible, if far fetched, contextualisation for *The dog scattered*. The deviance would seem, therefore, to be lexical rather than grammatical. But I am not really sure. Can we say *The dog scattered* even in such a context? Or would *The dog scattered itself* be more appropriate? My indecision here shows that we are on the borderline of grammar and lexicon.

6.4 *Grammatical relations*

Traditional grammars make great use of the notions of subject and object (and also of the distinction between direct and indirect object). This is largely based upon the formal distinctions of noun phrases within a sentence such as *John gave Bill a book*, where *John* is subject, *Bill* indirect object and *a book* direct object, and these are defined by the position of the noun phrases relative to the verb and to one another. In Latin these grammatical relations, as they have been called, are marked by inflection – by the case (in the traditional sense, not Fillmore's) of the nouns, the subject being in the nominative, the direct object in the accusative and the indirect object in the dative, as in *Marcus* (nom.) *librum* (acc.) *Julio* (dat.) *dedit* 'Marcus gave Julius a book'.

These grammatical relations are also important when we consider the category of voice (active and passive) in many languages. For, if we compare *John played the piano* and *The piano was played by John*, it is apparent that, while *the piano* is the object in the first sentence, which is active, it is the subject in the second, the passive, while *John* is the subject in the first, but appears after *by* in the second. Intuitively, and informally, what we want to say is that the object of the active sentence becomes the subject of the passive, while the subject moves to the position after *by* or becomes the 'agent'. If we think in terms of deep structures, we could regard *John* as the deep subject and *the piano* as the deep object, and allow the transformational rules to place them in their correct (but different) position in the surface structures of the active and passive sentences (though in the active sentences the subjects and objects will be in the same position in both deep and surface structure).

There are, however, some complications. In English we find that the indirect object may become the subject of the passive, as in *Bill was given a book by John*, as may the direct object – *A book was given to Bill by John* (though this might perhaps be seen as the passive of *John gave a book to Bill* not *John gave Bill a book*). Moreover, we find sentences such as *The old man was looked after by his daughter* in which *the old man* is not strictly the object of the sentence in the active, but is preceded by the preposition *after*; the solution here is to see *look after* as a single verb. More idiosyncratic is *The bed's not been slept in* in which *sleep in* again seems to function as a unit (but contrast the unlikely **The office's not been worked in*). However, we must obviously make special statements for sentences of this kind. In general, the rule about transformations, which involves movement of subject and object, holds good.

As long as the terms 'deep subject' and 'deep object' are used to deal solely with formal relations of this kind no real problems arise. But we may well be tempted to see the deep subject as the 'doer' and the deep object as the 'sufferer'; some linguists have used the terms ACTOR and GOAL to make this distinction. There are, however, difficulties if we attempt to define them in semantic terms. For it is by no means true that the subject of a transitive verb can always be seen as one who 'does' something. There are many verbs in English that are not verbs of action but of state, e.g. *like* in *I like ice cream* or even *see* in *I saw the boys*. Indeed with some of these verbs we should not usually ask *What did he do?* (though this, contrary to what some linguists have suggested, is not a very clear test, as the reader can judge for himself with *like* and *see*). Verbs of this kind should deter us from attempting to define *actor* in semantic terms. But even with action verbs, it is not clear that we can clearly establish what is meant by *actor*. For instance, Halliday (1970: 147) quotes as an example of an actor *General Leathwell* in the sentence *General Leathwell won the battle*. But in what sense is he the actor? Did he fire any guns, kill any enemy, advance to the enemy's lines, or did he merely sit in his HQ and let the troops get on with the battle? We could surely argue that semantically he was not the actor, but the 'supervisor'!

In spite of the absence of any clear semantic definitions for these grammatical relations some scholars, those who have advocated RELATIONAL GRAMMAR, have argued that they are universal and subject to certain rules. (Although we have talked about deep 'subjects' and 'objects', this was only an informal description and restricted solely to English – and Chomsky actually saw no reason to use these terms.) One of the main arguments is that the formal differences between active and passive sentences vary considerably in different languages. Although many of them have transformations involving movement of noun phrases, the movements are different, while some languages do not in fact move the noun phrases at all, e.g. Hindi *Ram ne moter celai* 'Ram drove the car', *Ram se moter celai gei* 'The car was driven by Ram' (Johnson 1974: 271). It is only in terms of subject and object that we can make any general, universal statements about active and passive. For, whatever the apparent differences in the various languages, in all cases the object of the active becomes the subject of the passive and the subject of the active is removed elsewhere.

Most of the arguments in favour of relational grammar are of a technical and syntactic nature, ranging over numerous languages, and cannot be followed up here. But, in general, it seems to be the case that such notions as subject and object are useful in many languages. However, there are some languages which appear to have a different system of grammatical relations. One of the most obvious facts about subject and object in languages like English is that some verbs, those that are transitive, typically have both subjects and objects (e.g. *hit* in *John hit Bill*), while others, the intransitive verbs, have subjects only (e.g. *fall* in *John fell*). In talking about the noun phrase with the intransitive verb as 'subject' we are, of course, identifying it, in relational terms, with the subject of the transitive verb, and the justification is found in formal features of the language (pre-verb position in English, nominative case in Latin). But there are some languages, the so-called 'ergative' languages, such as Basque, Eskimo and Georgian, in which the noun phrase with the intransitive verb is identified with what we would regard as the 'object' of the transitive verb. In these languages the 'subject' of the intransitive verb and the 'object' of the transitive verb are in the same case, the nominative or the absolutive, while the subject of the transitive verb is in the ergative case. ('Subject' and 'object' are in quotation marks because the whole point about the ergative languages is that these terms are inappropriate to them and can only be interpreted by reference to the 'transitive' languages such as English.) A pair of examples from Basque is *gizonak jo du chakurra* 'the man has beaten the dog' and *gizona dator* 'the man has come'; here *chakurra* ('dog') in the first sentence and *gizona* ('man') in the second are in the same (nominative) case, while *gizonak* ('man') in the first is marked by the suffix *-k* as ergative.

There are some languages, e.g. some of the Semitic languages that have formal devices to mark CAUSATIVITY. Thus Tigrinya (Ethiopia) has *zäkkäre* 'he remembered' and *'azäkkäre* 'he reminded (someone)', where the prefix *'a-* is the mark of the causative. This is of interest to us here because the distinction involved sometimes corresponds to that of intransitive and transitive in English. Thus the contrast between intransitive and transitive *bounce* in English is found in the basic (non-causative) and causative forms of the verb meaning 'jump'. French and many other languages in a similar way use a verb meaning 'do' or 'make': English intransitive and transitive *cook* are translated into French by *cuire* and *faire cuire*. (English, too, has a few causative forms, though only in a historical sense, e.g. *fell* in *He felled the tree* = 'He caused the tree to fall'.)

Some linguists have suggested that the transitivity distinction can be dealt with in terms of causativity, the transitive being seen as the causative of a basic non-causative form. Thus *John rang the bell* is interpreted as 'John caused the bell to ring' and, by an extension of this idea, *John killed Bill* as 'John caused Bill to die'. But there are objections to this. First, there is a difference between this purely semantic analysis of English and the formal features of Tigrinya and French (though this might not disturb the advocates of generative semantics – see 6.1). Secondly, languages have causatives of transitive as well as (basically) intransitive verbs. Tigrinya has *säbbäre* 'he broke (something)' and *'asbäre* 'he caused (someone) to break (something)', while both Tigrinya and Italian would translate English *show* by what is literally 'cause (someone) to see'. Moreover, there seems to be no obvious motivation for the choice of the intransitive or the transitive as the basic non-causative form. Tigrinya does not, as we might have expected from the arguments about English, treat the intransitive 'break' as basic and the transitive as causative; the intransitive is, in fact, indicated by a form with the passive prefix – *täsäbre*. Nor does Tigrinya relate 'die' and 'kill' in terms of the formal distinction. More surprisingly, in Classical Greek 'kill' seems to be more basic than 'die', for one can 'die by someone'; this would suggest that 'die' is the passive of 'kill', rather than that 'kill' is the causative of 'die'.

Furthermore, there are degrees of plausibility in the causative analysis of English verbs. A causative analysis of *march* in *The sergeant marched the recruits* is more reasonable than a similar analysis of (transitive) *ring* or *kill*. It is clear that the recruits actively performed the action of marching and that the sergeant caused them to do so, but bells that are rung and people who are killed do not actively perform the actions of ringing and dying under causation. Even less attractive is a causative analysis of transitive *hit*, for although we may paraphrase the other examples ('John caused the bell to ring', 'John caused Bill to die'), there is no similar paraphrase for *John hit Bill* – 'John caused Bill to — (?)'.

6.5 *Components and the sentence*

We have already seen how components may be used to state

selectional restrictions. All that is needed is that a particular component should be stated as a feature of one of the collocated words and as part of the required environment of the other. Thus *beer*, but not *bread*, has the component (liquid), and it is stated for *drink* that part of its required environment is a following noun with that component. By this means we can rule out **John drank the bread*. We can also disambiguate: only *bank* in the sense of a financial institution will be possible in *a wealthy bank*, since *wealthy* will be shown as occurring only with a noun that has certain components, e.g. (human), (institutional), etc.

Katz & Fodor (1963), however, suggest that we can go further and actually derive the meaning of a sentence from the meaning of the words it contains. It is worthwhile looking in detail at their model if only to illustrate how difficult it is to move from word to sentence meaning, and because no one else has made such a clear and detailed proposal. In simple language what they propose is a set of rules to combine the meanings of individual lexical items. The rules are called PROJECTION RULES, the combination is referred to as AMALGAMATION, and the meanings are called PATHS. The paths are no more than the structural analysis of the meaning as shown in Figure 6 (5.7) – and the amalgamation is thus a combination of the markers and distinguishers. Projection rules are needed since it is necessary to state what may be amalgamated with what, and in what order. This will be determined by the grammatical status of the elements – we shall combine adjective with noun, noun phrase with verb, and so on.

The example chosen by Katz & Fodor as an illustration of the application of the projection rules is *The man hit the colorful ball* (since I use their example, I will retain the American spelling). We must first establish the grammatical status of the lexical items, that *colorful* is an adjective and *ball* a noun and that together with *the* they form a noun phrase, and so on, but we need not bother with the details here. We then have to amalgamate the paths of the various lexical items. We begin with *colorful* and *ball*. In one path for *colorful* we find a marker (color) referring to actual colour, but there is another path in which the marker is (evaluative) to deal with the meaning of *colorful* to refer to the colourful nature of any aesthetic object. *Ball* has three paths, one with the marker (social activity), the other two with the marker (physical object) but distinguished by the distinguishers [having globular shape] and [solid missile for projection by engine of war]. We are concerned, that is to say, with the ball at which people dance, the 'ordinary' round ball and cannon balls. (There is much more information not relevant for our purpose.) But there is a further and vital piece of information; the first *colorful* is specified as occurring in the environment of either (physical object) or (social activity), the second in the environment of either (aesthetic object) – this is, in fact, irrelevant for us – or (social activity). Although we have three paths for *ball* and two for *colorful*, when we amalgamate their paths to produce *colorful ball* we shall not have six (three times two) amalgamated paths, but only four. The reason is, of course, that the second path of *colorful* (evaluative) will not amalgamate with that of *ball* with the marker (physical object). In general terms we are saying that all three balls can be colourful in the literal sense of having colour, but only the ball at which people dance can be colourful in the evaluative sense – the other two balls cannot. (I am not concerned with the factual accuracy of these statements, only with them as examples.)

We now amalgamate *colorful ball* with *hit*. *Hit* has two paths, one indicating collision, the other indicating striking, and both occur in the environment (physical object). We shall not, however, now have eight (two times four) derived paths, since neither will amalgamate with *colorful ball* with the marker (social activity), since in neither sense of *hit* can this kind of ball be hit. We shall instead have only four possibilities. Finally, we can amalgamate the path of *The man* (one path only), and so eventually derive four readings only for the sentence (colliding with or striking either an ordinary ball or a cannon ball).

In our previous discussion we saw roughly how componential analysis has been used to deal with anomalies and selectional restrictions. More precisely, projection rules handle such sentences as *The idea cut the tree* or *John drank the bread* by assigning them no readings at all. Just as some of the amalgamated paths are ruled out for *The man hit the colorful ball*, so all paths are ruled out for these anomalous sentences and no readings result. Indeed, an anomalous sentence is to be DEFINED as one that has no readings. We have seen some of the problems with componential analysis in general and with its use in dealing with selectional restrictions. But there are further difficulties in the attempt to use it to move from word to sentence.

First, if we merely add components together as we use the projection rules then it will follow that *Cats chase mice* and *Mice chase cats* have exactly the same meaning. The point is clear – *chase* is essentially relational, just as are the relational opposites of 5.5. Indeed the active/passive relationship is essentially one of relational opposites since *Cats chase mice* entails *Mice are chased by cats*. The 'direction' of the relation is important and has to be stated. As we saw in 5.7 it is possible to 'insert' direction into components, but that is essentially to treat them not as components, but as relations.

Secondly, a problem arises in that the same component may at times merely provide the environment for amalgamation, at others be part of the derived path (i.e. part of the meaning of the resultant combination). Consider the word *pregnant*. If we follow the procedure for *colorful ball* we shall wish to say that this will occur only in the environment of (−male) so as to permit *pregnant woman*, but not *pregnant man*. But we can also say *pregnant horse*, though *horse* (unlike *mare*) is not marked (−male) and, moreover, *pregnant horse* clearly refers to a female creature and can be combined with . . . *gave birth*. In such an example the (−male) component has come from the adjective not the noun, yet the rules will have made no provision for this (nor can they very easily if, in general, we wish to treat *pregnant* as compatible only with female nouns). There are many other similar examples – *pretty child, buxom neighbour*, where the noun phrase is presumably (−male) but the nouns *child* and *neighbour* are not. Of course, ways can be found to deal with a problem such as this; one way (Weinreich 1966: 429–32) is to talk about a 'transfer feature' which can be transferred to another word. But such examples show that componential analysis does not provide a simple way of proceeding from the meaning of lexical items to the meaning of sentences by a process of the adding together of the components through amalgamation.

6.6 *Predicates and arguments*

We have already noted that in a sentence the verb is often best seen as a relational feature and, indeed, that active and passive sentences could be handled as if they were relational opposites (5.5). Analysis in relational terms seems to offer a far more satisfactory solution to the problem of sentence meaning than componential analysis. In essence such analysis will have much in common with predicate calculus, which we have already briefly introduced in 5.1, and shall be discussing in more detail in 8.3.

Since we are not concerned here with entailment or any other logical relation between sentences, we do not need formulae that express propositions, but can use what logicians call 'open sentences'. Thus we can characterise *walk*, *love* and *give* in terms of one- two- and three-place predicates – $W(x)$, $L(x,y)$ and $G(x,y,z)$. (To convert such open sentences into sentences expressing a proposition, we must either replace the variables x, y, z with constants, e.g. $W(a)$ 'John walks', or add a quantifier, e.g. $\forall x(W(x))$ 'Everyone walks'.) It will often be convenient to spell out the predicate in full with the relevant English word; when this is done it will be placed in square brackets – $[\text{Walk}](x)$, $[\text{Love}](x,y)$, $[\text{Give}](x,y,z)$. A major advantage of this approach is that it can handle 'atomic' components as well as relational ones. For we may regard such components as a relation involving just one argument. Let us take *father* as an example. Here we want to express both the relation of 'parent of' and the component (+male). This can be symbolised as [Parent] (x,y) & $M(x)$.

Predicate calculus provides a simple method of dealing with what is known in grammar as SUBORDINATION, by allowing a proposition to function as an argument. Thus we may wish to analyse *Fred thinks that John loves Mary* by saying that the predicate [Think] has two arguments, *Fred* and the proposition *John loves Mary*. We need to indicate that the whole proposition *John loves Mary* is one of the arguments of [Think]. The structure of this sentence can be given as [Think]$(x,([Love](y,z)))$, where the round brackets show that $([Love](y,z))$ is a single element, and like x, one of the arguments of [Think]. This illustrates that a proposition with its own predicate and arguments can also be an argument of another 'higher' proposition.

In these examples the semantic interpretation has not been very different from that suggested by the syntax of the sentence. But it is possible to break propositions down into far more basic elements than those indicated by the actual words of the sentence. For instance, we might think of treating *Bill gave Harry a book* in terms of a three-place predicate [Give] – [Give](x,y,z). But we could, instead, interpret the sentence as 'Bill caused Harry to have a book'. The formula then becomes [Cause]$(x,([Have](y,z)))$, where the arguments of [Cause] are (x) ('Bill') and [Have](y,z) ('Harry have a book'). Similarly we might treat *kill* as 'cause to die' or 'cause to become not alive'. The latter is more favoured, but it also involves the use of the logical operator $\sim$ 'not'. The formula for *John killed Mary* would then be [Cause]$(x, ([Become](y,([\sim Alive](y)))))$ i.e. 'John caused Mary become Mary not alive'; notice that both [Cause] and [Become] have a proposition as their second argument.

This kind of analysis is often written out in 'tree diagrams' which are used for syntax. Thus for our last example see Figure 7. The generative semanticists (see 6.3) argued that a representation of this kind did not merely relate to the

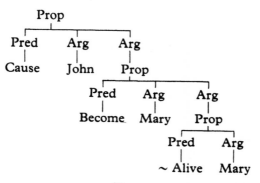

Figure 7

semantics of *kill*, but was rather its deep structure. The argument was largely based upon the triple ambiguity of *I almost killed him*, where, it is argued, *almost* may qualify *cause*, *become* or *not alive* (cf. Morgan 1969). The first sense applies if I shot at him, but missed (I almost caused the subsequent events, but did not). The second applies if I hit him and he recovered after narrowly avoiding death (he almost became dead). The third applies if I shot him and he was in a state of near death (he became almost dead). On the basis of this it is argued that *kill* must be interpreted in terms of three sentences in deep structure, for this will make it possible to place *almost* in each of these three sentences and thus show whether it qualifies *cause*, *become* or *not alive*.

It is a mistake, however, to confuse such a semantic representation with the syntax of a sentence. In particular *John killed Mary* is not identical with *John caused Mary to become not alive*, since it is (just) possible to say *On Thursday John caused Mary to become not alive on Saturday* but not *On Thursday John killed Mary on Saturday*. The difference lies in the temporal marking of the predicates, and if there is only one verb in the original sentence there cannot be more than one time indication. We have not discussed tense and time, nor can we now do so, but clearly they (as well as all the semantics of place, manner, etc.) have eventually to be accounted for.

6.7 *Case grammar*

Case grammar was first proposed by Fillmore (1968) as one of
the arguments in favour of generative semantics (see 6.1), but
is best understood as a version of an analysis in terms of
predicates and arguments, in which the emphasis is largely
upon the functions of the arguments.

A good starting point is the trio of sentences *John opened
the door with a key*, *The key opened the door* and *The door
opened*. There is the same verb, *open*, in all three, and in all
three it is active. Yet the grammatical subjects are *John*, *the
key* and *the door* respectively. We can account for these facts if
we treat *open* as the predicate, *John*, *the key* and *the door* as the
arguments and if, further, we handle *John*, *the key* and *the
door* in terms of 'case relations' that are not directly related to
grammatical subject and object, the case of each noun being
the same in all three sentences. Thus *John* is AGENTIVE
(='actor') throughout, *the key* is INSTRUMENTAL and *the door*
is OBJECTIVE. Similar sets of sentences, and similar analyses,
can be provided for other verbs; e.g. *break* or *ring*: *John broke
the window with a stone*, *The stone broke the window*, *The
window broke*. But the categories would still be formal –
based only on relations of a transformational kind between
sentences.

Fillmore suggests that his case notions are 'a set of universal, presumably innate, concepts' and proceeds to define
them in semantic terms. To begin with he suggests six cases,
AGENTIVE ('typically animate perceived instigator'), IN-
STRUMENTAL ('inanimate force or object causally involved'),
DATIVE ('animate being affected'), FACTITIVE ('object or being
resulting from the action or state'), LOCATIVE ('location
or spatial orientation'), OBJECTIVE ('the semantically most
neutral case'). In a later work (Fillmore 1971a), we find
dative renamed EXPERIENCER and factitive being replaced by
RESULT, with the addition of COUNTER-AGENT ('the force or
resistance against which the action is carried out'), SOURCE
('the place from which something moves') and GOAL ('the

place to which something moves'); in addition he talks of 'agents', 'objects', etc., instead of 'agentive', 'objective'.

The argument for case relations is not restricted to verbs such as *open*. It is suggested that the converse relationship of *teach* and *learn* can be accounted for in *John taught French to Mary, Mary learnt French from John*, by treating *John* as the agent, *Mary* as the experiencer and *French* as the object. Similarly *show* needs agent, experiencer and object (one shows something to somebody), while *see* requires experiencer and object. There is a contrast between *see* and *look* (*at*), in that the latter requires agent and object (with *look* the person takes an active part, with *see* he is merely affected).

Case grammar, it is argued, can easily account for the difference between *John ruined the table* and *John built the table*. In the first *the table* is the object; in the second it is the result. More strikingly, we can account for the supposed ambiguity of *Peter broke the window* (deliberately or accidentally) by assigning *Peter* to the agent on the one meaning and to the instrument on the other.

As we saw at the beginning, there is no one-to-one correspondence between case and the grammatical subject or object. In our first set of examples the agent (*John*), the object (*the door*) and the instrument (*the key*) all occurred as grammatical subjects. Similarly, the location may be the subject as in *Chicago is windy* (cf. *It is windy in Chicago*), as may the experiencer in *John believed that he would win* (cf. *It was apparent to John that he would win*). There are, moreover, some rules governing what case will 'surface' as the subject. To begin with, we cannot conjoin two different cases and so cannot say **John and the key opened the door*. Secondly, there is a hierarchical ordering of the cases which is, in part, agent > experiencer > instrument > object. This ensures that with *open*, if the agent (*John*) is present it will be the subject – *John opened the door with a key*, but not **The key opened the door by John* or **The door opened with a key by John*. Similarly if there is an instrument but no agent, the instrument will be the subject – *The key opened the door*, but not **The door opened* *with a key*. Only if the object is alone can it be the subject – *The door opened*. As a means of relating sentences such as these, case grammar works well. We could easily produce a comparable set with *ring* – *John rang the bell with a hammer*, *The hammer rang the bell*, *The bell rang*. This ordering is, however, overruled by a transformation such as the passive, where the object will be the grammatical subject (*The door was opened by John with a key*), or with certain lexically defined verbs, e.g. *please*, where the object is again the grammatical subject, although the experiencer is present, e.g. *This pleases me*.

One major difficulty that seemed to face the early version of case grammar was that it was apparently unable to distinguish between such sentences as *John smeared the wall with paint* and *John smeared paint on the wall*, or between *John sold a book to Henry* and *Henry bought a book from John*. Fillmore suggests, in a later work (1977: 60), that this is a matter of PERSPECTIVE. In our first examples either *the wall* or *the paint* are brought into perspective. With *buy* and *sell* we have the buyer, the seller, the goods and the money, and all can be brought into perspective by the choice of verb, for we have not only *buy* and *sell*, but also *pay* (*Henry paid five dollars for the book*) and *cost* (*The book cost five dollars*).

Case grammar is attractive in many ways, but, as the last paragraph shows, the deeper the investigation, the more complex it seems to become. Moreover, there are still plenty of problems. The suggestion that the supposed ambiguity of *Peter broke the window* is explained by treating Peter as either experiencer or agent seems to be invalid, for we can say *Peter and Bill both broke the window*, *Peter accidentally and Bill on purpose*, and we were told that two different cases could not be conjoined. However, the fact that we cannot conjoin does not seem to be wholly determined by case: **I saw Helen and a football match* is a very strange sentence, yet both *Helen* and *a football match* are here in the object case.

Moreover, case grammar runs into the familiar difficulty of the vagueness of semantic categories. Often it will be difficult to decide, on semantic grounds, what is the case of a particular noun phrase. Fillmore sees *the smoke* as object in *The smoke rose*, and the same would be true of *the wind* in *The wind blew*. But what, then, shall we say of *The smoke rose and blotted out the sun*, *The wind blew and opened the door*? Apart from the fact that both *the smoke* and *the wind* are probably simultaneously in two different cases, it seems more reasonable to regard *the smoke* as instrument than *the wind*, since the smoke was probably moved by the wind. Moreover, it is not easy to see why *the wind* is instrument rather than agent. Animacy and deliberateness have both been suggested as tests of what is agent, and these would rule out *the wind*. But it would be difficult to reach a similar decision with *The virus killed the organism* or even *The slugs destroyed the cabbages*. (Did they do so deliberately?!) A particularly difficult problem is *My ear is twitching*. *My ear* could be agent since it is 'doing' the twitching, or experiencer, or even location (*I have a twitch in my ear*). It is difficult to see how, even in principle, we can decide, and there is clearly a danger of ever increasing the distinctions and the criteria for them.

6.8 *Sentence types and modality*

Although it has been pointed out several times (e.g. 2.5) that language does not consist solely of statements, much of what has been said so far, has, in fact, related to declarative sentences, sentences that are typically used to make statements and so belong essentially to the descriptive aspect of language.

We clearly do not simply make statements, we also ask questions and give commands. This threefold distinction, moreover, seems to be reflected in the grammar of the languages with which we are familiar: English clearly distinguishes:

John shut the door.
Did John shut the door?
Shut the door.

We can refer to these as DECLARATIVE, INTERROGATIVE and IMPERATIVE sentences respectively; they are formally distinguished in English, the interrogative being marked by inversion of the verb and subject, and, in certain grammatical contexts, by the introduction of the auxiliary verb *do*, the imperative by omission of the subject and by absence of tense marking. But we should be warned by the discussion of formal grammar (6.1) not to expect a one-to-one correspondence between the grammatically defined sentence types and their function. That declarative, interrogative and imperative sentences do not respectively give information, ask for information and request action, is clearly shown by the following:

(1) *I want to know where you have been.*
    I insist that you stay.
(2) *Have you heard the news that we won?*
    Haven't I told you not to do that?
(3) *Understand that I can't do that.*
    Tell me what you have done.

It would be useful, therefore, to restrict the use of *declarative, interrogative* and *imperative* to the description of these sentences types, and to use *statement, question* and *command* for the functions. The (1) sentences are declaratives but not statements, the (2) sentences interrogatives but not questions and the (3) sentences imperatives but not commands (cf. Bar-Hillel 1970: 365).

The distinction we have just made is essentially one between sentence meaning and utterance meaning (2.5), but it is not always easy to make the distinction. For what are we to say of a sentence such as *John's coming?* with a rising intonation. We could argue that this is declarative though a question, or we could say that the intonation is a formal mark of the interrogative, just as the inversion of subject and verb auxiliary is. While there is some attraction in trying to incorporate intonational features into grammar (see 7.1), this will almost certainly create far too many problems. For *John's coming* may be uttered with many intonation tunes, and it would be virtually impossible to assign a grammatical function to all of these, even though some often have a fairly constant meaning. The fall-rise, for instance, usually says 'but . . .' as in *He's very ˇclever* which might be taken to imply 'but he's not very nice'. Whether the rising intonation is to be associated with 'interrogative' or with 'question' is a matter for debate.

A further problem arises with a sentence such as *Can you pass the salt?* At first it may seem obvious that this is an interrogative, but with the function of a command. But it often occurs with *please – Can you pass the salt please?*, and this would suggest that it is being marked in the language as a command. Moreover, we cannot make a similar request with *Are you able to pass the salt?* Clearly the sentence is to some degree conventionally determined, and it is important that *can* and not *be able to* is used. There is at least some plausibility in saying that such sentences are imperatives rather than interrogatives. We shall return to this problem again later (7.3 and 7.5).

Some linguists have used the term MOOD to refer to the distinction of declarative/interrogative/imperative. This is not altogether inappropriate for English, but is not in accordance with the traditional grammarians' use of the term, which usually relates to the indicative, subjunctive and imperative moods that are marked inflectionally in Latin and other languages (see e.g. Palmer 1971: 93–4). The interrogative is not a mood in this sense. But this three-term Latin distinction (or four-term if we consider Classical Greek, which also has an optative mood) is not reflected in many languages of the world. Some have a large range of different forms indicating all kinds of difference of meaning. Thus Bilin uses inflection to indicate time (past, present, future), conditionals, 'when', 'while', reported speech, etc. Whether we use the term *mood* or the term *tense* to refer to these forms, or find another name is a purely terminological question.

More relevant to the issue of mood (more narrowly defined) is the situation in Hidatsa, a North American Indian language (Matthews 1965: 99–101). Here every sentence contains one of a set of six particles or 'mood morphemes'. 'In general', says Matthews, 'the moods indicate the truth value of the sentence.' The six are as follows, with Matthews' glosses:

Emphatic: 'indicates that the speaker knows the sentence to be true: if a sentence that ends with the Emphatic mood is false, the speaker is considered a liar'.

Period: 'indicates that the speaker believes the sentence to be true: if it should turn out otherwise it would mean that he was mistaken, but by no means a liar'.

Quotative: 'indicates that the speaker regards what he has said to be something that everyone knows'.

Report: 'indicates that the speaker was told the information given in the sentence by someone else, but has no evidence of its truth value'.

Indefinite/Question: 'both indicate that the speaker does not know whether or not the sentence is true. The Indefinite also means that the speaker thinks the listener does know'.

The most remarkable point about Hidatsa is that it is not possible to make what we might call an 'unmodalised' statement at all. The grammar of the language forces the speaker to indicate what is the status of what is being said, in exactly the same way as the grammars of European languages usually compel speakers to indicate the time at which the relevant events took place.

Yet English, too, has ways of expressing degrees and kinds of commitment by the speaker, most obviously in the use of the so-called 'modal verbs' *will, shall, can, may, must* and *ought to*. We can distinguish in their use several kinds of modality (using the term *modality* to refer to function, while *mood* is defined in terms of grammatical form (cf.

Palmer 1979: 4)). First, there is what has been called EPI-
STEMIC modality which expresses the degree of commitment
of the speaker to the truth of what is being said. Thus we can
distinguish between *He may/must/will be in his office.* These
may be roughly paraphrased: 'It is possible that . . .', 'The
only possible conclusion is that . . .', 'A reasonable conclusion is that. . .'. Secondly, the modal verbs are used for
DEONTIC modality which has much in common with the
imperative. The speaker can give permission, lay an obligation or give an undertaking, in relation to possible future
events with e.g. *You may* (or *can*) */must/shall come tomorrow.*
Thus, while epistemic modality is concerned with the
speaker's relation to propositions, deontic modality is concerned with his active relation to events. (But here *deontic* is
defined more narrowly than is usual – see Palmer 1979:
58–9.)

As the use of the term *modality* is intended to suggest,
these do not correspond to any clear grammatical distinction.
Indeed, some uses of the modal verbs, e.g. *can* to express
ability (*He can run a mile in four minutes*) or *will* for willing-
ness (*He won't do as I ask*), are not really expressions of
modality at all. Nevertheless, there are two points to note.
First, it is normally only with epistemic modality that the
modals occur with *have* – to express judgments about the
past, *He may/must/will have been in his office* (except for *ought
to have* and a 'future perfect' use of *will have*). Secondly,
alongside *may* and *can*, English has *be able to*, and alongside
must it has *have (got) to*; one clear difference is that the other
verbs do not normally express either type of modality. It can
even be argued that the essential difference between *will* and
be going to is that one expresses a modal, the other a non-
modal future (Palmer 1979: 108ff.).

The chief moral of this section is that we should not think
that the main or only function of language is to make statements. We also ask questions, give commands, etc., and in
various ways in various languages the speaker can (or even
must) express his commitment or attitude to what is being

said. But the discussion of mood and modality, and especially that of the English modals, illustrates a further point – that we cannot draw a very clear line between sentence meaning and utterance meaning. That is then a useful point on which to end this chapter and begin the next.

7

UTTERANCE MEANING

In this chapter we shall be discussing several kinds of meaning that are not directly related to the grammatical structure of the sentence. Nevertheless, the choice of the title of this chapter does not assume that a clear distinction can be made between utterance meaning and sentence meaning – see 2.5 and the concluding remarks of the last chapter.

7.1 *The spoken language*

One important characteristic of the linguistic approach towards the study of language is that it is not concerned merely with the written language, but also (and usually with greater emphasis) with the spoken. There are at least four ways in which the spoken language is 'prior to', or more basic than, the written:

(1) The human race had speech long before it had writing and there are still many languages that have no written form.
(2) The child learns to speak long before he learns to write.
(3) Speech plays a far greater role in our lives than writing. We spend far more time speaking than writing or reading.
(4) Written language can, to a large extent, be converted into speech without loss. But the converse is not true; if we write down what is said we lose a great deal.

The fourth point is one that needs further discussion. There are some features of the written form that are not easily (or not at all) represented in speech. For instance, the use of italics in this book to refer to examples would not be indicated if it were read aloud. Nor would the paragraphs, though that might not be a great loss. But the spoken language has far more striking characteristics that cannot be easily shown in the written form. In particular it has prosodic and paralinguistic features (see 2.5). The prosodic features include primarily what is usually handled under intonation and stress. We have already briefly discussed (6.8), the use of a rising intonation to indicate a question and that of a fall-rise to suggest 'but . . .', and any speaker of English can easily become aware of the great use made of intonation for a whole variety of purposes, largely of an attitudinal kind.

It would be quite impossible to do justice to the meaning of these prosodic and paralinguistic features in a book of this size. The exposition of the formal characteristics of these features is a major exercise in itself (cf. Crystal 1969) and the way in which they relate in detail to meaning has still not been fully explained, and, indeed, it must be accepted that there is no simple one-to-one relation between any of these features and any very specific meaning or function. We can, nevertheless, point out a few characteristics of the prosodic systems that have fairly regular functions.

A very simple, if not simplistic, view of stress and intonation in English sees the intonational pattern of a stretch of speech as consisting of a number of intonation tunes or 'tone groups' (O'Connor & Arnold 1961: 29), each of which has a nucleus, in which there is a considerable movement of pitch, largely within a single syllable of a word. The direction of the pitch movement varies and this allows us to recognise different basic intonation tunes, fall, fall-rise, rise, etc. (Crystal 1969: 225). Moreover, the nucleus may occur in different places – in different words within the tune. With a rising intonation, being used for a question, for instance, it may occur on any of the words in *Is Mary going to wear that hat?* This is sometimes referred to as sentence stress or ACCENT (but in a different sense, of course, from that of the different regional 'accents' that are associated with different dialects).

The tune or tone group will sometimes correspond with the clause in English, and we should normally expect two tone groups in a sentence such as *If John comes, I shall not be here*. But we should find only one tone group with *John said that he wasn't coming*, even though here, too, there are two clauses. In any case there is no absolute rule; the tone group is probably determined primarily by what the speaker regards as an information unit, and this may overrule the grammatical considerations. Moreover, there are also some conventions that create a striking mismatch between the grammatical and intonational units. For instance, it would be quite normal to say *I'm not going out. It's too cold* on a single tune (probably a fall), although there are clearly two sentences here. But the use of a single tune indicates the close, causal connection between these two sentences.

Different tunes may, as we have already seen, be associated with different functions – a rise with a question and the fall-rise with the implication 'but . . .' (but see 7.5). Falls are associated more with statements, though a more casual or tentative statement can occur with a rise. There are no absolute rules, and some conventions go against the general trend. For instance 'wh-questions' (those with *who, what, why, when, how,* etc.) normally occur, not with the rise associated with a question, but with a fall.

The place of the nucleus is more directly relevant to us. It is determined by features of topic and comment (7.2) and, therefore, also apparently related to some questions of presupposition (7.4). This we shall discuss in the appropriate sections.

There is, however, very much more. With other variations in the intonation tune the speaker can express emotions, attitudes, etc., and indeed this is a more typical usage of intonation. Some of the conventions clearly vary from dialect to dialect, and it seems likely that many of the misunderstandings between, for instance, English and Americans is due to the fact that they have different interpretations of the same intonational features.

Even apart from the prosodic and paralinguistic features, we have to recognise that the form of spoken language and the purposes for which it is used are very different from those of the written. Concentration on the written language has misled grammarians – they have often failed to see that the spoken language is different from the written and have, misleadingly, attempted to describe the spoken language in terms appropriate to the written. It has been even more misleading for semanticists. For the written language is largely narration or the presentation of factual information or arguments. This has led to the assumption that meaning is largely concerned with information, or with propositions (see 2.5). But the main function of language, especially the spoken language, is not to inform. It performs many other quite different functions.

7.2 *Topic and comment*

A number of Czech linguists, e.g. Firbas (1959, 1964) and Daneš (1968), have for some time been interested in Functional Sentence Perspective or FSP, for short. In particular, they have distinguished in the sentence between THEME and RHEME, or what has in most other schools of linguistics been called TOPIC and COMMENT. This stems from the idea that we can distinguish between what we are talking about (the topic) and what we are saying about it (the comment). In some languages, there are formal ways of distinguishing topic and comment – and the category is thus a formal one. One way in which the distinction may be made is by the order of the words, and this is the situation in Czech where the theme, what is being talked about, is placed in initial position in the sentence.

If a language has clear markers of topic and comment, the linguistic description raises few problems, for the categories are formally marked and it is always relatively easy to give semantic descriptions to formal categories. But English and many other languages have no simple formal category and it is then not clear what might be meant by *topic* and *comment*.

Indeed in English there seem to be at least four features that can be related to the notion.

First, it is possible in English to place a word at the beginning of a sentence when this is not its normal syntactic position as in *The man over there I do not like very much*. This is a device for indicating first what we are going to talk about, and is thus reasonably treated as an example of topicalisation. But it is a fairly rare phenomenon in English. We do not usually place words or phrases initially for this purpose. Moreover, if this is topic, it is marked only if the words or phrases are NOT in their normal positions.

Secondly, we can often choose alternative syntactic constructions whose chief difference lies in what is the subject. An obvious example is active and passive, *John hit Bill* and *Bill was hit by John*. More complex are *This violin is easy to play sonatas on*, *Sonatas are easy to play on this violin*. It has been argued (Chomsky 1971: 209; Jackendoff 1972: 227) that the choice is determined by topicalisation, the construction chosen being the one which brings the topic into subject position. But it is by no means clear that *John* and *Bill*, *the violin* and *sonatas* are in any independent semantic sense the topic, or what is being 'talked about'. There is a danger of circularity here – of saying that a particular noun is chosen as subject because it is the topic, but then having no way of identifying the topic except as the subject. We ought to look for some clear motivation for the choice of one construction rather than another with particular reference to the choice of the subject. There are, perhaps, two reasons for choosing the passive. First, it is often a matter of the 'cohesion' of the discourse to retain the same subject – *The child ran into the road and was hit by a car* shows a little more 'cohesion' than *The child ran into the road and a car hit him*. Secondly, the passive is used where the 'doer' is unknown as in *The child was knocked down*, or where it is deliberately left unstated. This is characteristic of scientific reports where the reporter uses the passive to avoid reference to himself, e.g. *The water was heated to 80°C*. But the first of these is little more than a stylistic device, and the second is a direct result of the grammar of English, which always requires a sentence to have a subject. Only in a very vague sense, then, is choice of construction involving the subject a matter of topicalisation.

Thirdly, English has clear devices for dealing with the GIVEN and the NEW, the information that is already known in the discourse and the information that is being freshly stated. English has several ways of making the distinction. We can avoid restating in detail what is given by using pronouns – the third person pronouns *he/she/it/they* instead of the already mentioned *the little boy*, *the man on the corner*, etc. Not only are there pronouns, there are also pro-verbs, e.g. *do* as in *John came early and so did Fred*, and there are, similarly, 'pro-form' adjectives, adverbs and conjunctions – *such*, *so*, *therefore*, etc. All of these refer back to something already stated, which is not, therefore, to be stated in full again. We also use sentence stress or accent for a similar purpose, the general rule being that the accent, the point at which there is a fall or a rise, will be on the last item that is new; whatever follows is given and is by this means not highlighted. Thus in *John hit Bill and then Fréd hit him* the accent falls on *Fred* since that alone is new, *hit* and *him* being part of what is given. In contrast in *John saw Bill and then Fred hít him* the accent will fall on *hit*, for *hit* is now new. It will follow from this that the accent will not normally fall upon a pronoun (but see the next paragraph for exceptions). It is, perhaps, significant that with the phrasal verbs a pronoun cannot occur at all in final position in the sentence. For, though we can say *He made up a story* and *He made a story up*, we cannot say *He made up it, but only *He made it up*. Sentence final position is, perhaps, too prominent, and thus inappropriate for what is so obviously given. The given, incidentally, may be given from the general, non-linguistic context, not the linguistic discourse. Thus in *The kettle's boiling* the accent usually falls on *kettle* simply because *boiling* is uninformative. There is nothing new, for what else could the kettle be doing?

Fourthly, we often use accent for contrast. In *John hit Bill* any one of the three words may be accented. But this is not merely to topicalise, but to contrast. We are not merely talking about John, hitting or Bill, but we are saying that it was John and not someone else, hitting and not something else, Bill and not someone else. Even more strikingly, we can place the accent on *him* in *John hit Bill and then Fred hit hím* to mean that Fred hit John not Bill. The explanation is that the accent on *hím* indicates contrast, i.e. 'not Bill', and the only possible inference is that it was John. There is a similar, though more striking use, with *not*, where the accent 'picks' out what or who 'is not'; in contrast with what or who 'is'. Thus we can accent various words in *The professors didn't sign the petition* to suggest that others did, that they did something other than sign, or that they signed something else. The same semantic effect can often be achieved by using the paraphrase *It was . . ., It was John who hit Bill, It wasn't the professors who signed the petition* (for the verb we have to say *What John did was to hit Bill*). But such paraphrases are not always possible, e.g. with a contrasted adjective or adverb – *He's not a crúel man, He didn't run fást*, for we cannot say **It isn't cruel that he's a man*, **It isn't fast that he ran*. Moreover, we can accent parts of words – *They didn't dénationalise (They re-nationalised)*, *This isn't a Sémitic language (It's Hamitic)*. No paraphrase at all is possible here. It has been suggested that these accentual differences may be handled in terms of deep structures based upon the paraphrases, but it is clear that this cannot work for all our examples.

We have, then, at least four different phenomena that may be handled under topic and comment. All are in their own way part of the semantics of the language.

7.3 *Performatives and speech acts*

In a famous little book, edited and published after his death, *How to do things with words* Austin (1962) pointed out that there are a number of utterances that do not report or 'con-state' anything and are not therefore 'true or false', but rather that the uttering of the sentence is, or is part of, an action.

Examples are *I name this ship Queen Elizabeth, I bet you sixpence it will rain tomorrow.* By uttering such sentences the speaker actually names the ship or makes the bet, but he is not making any kind of statement that can be regarded as true or false. The sentences that he is concerned with here are grammatically all statements, but they are not CONSTATIVE, they are PERFORMATIVE. Austin includes along with the performative sentences (or simply performatives) *I promise . . .* and suggests that one can find a list of performative verbs including *apologise, thank, censure, approve, congratulate.* With all of these a sentence with *I* and a present tense verb will be an example of a performative.

He proceeds to distinguish these performatives as EXPLICIT performatives in contrast with the IMPLICIT performatives which do not contain an expression naming the act. We can achieve the same end with *Go* as with *I order you to go* and similarly *There is a bull in the field* may (or may not) be a warning, while *I shall be there* may (or may not) be a promise. This leads to the distinction between a LOCUTIONARY ACT and an ILLOCUTIONARY ACT. In the locutionary act we are 'saying something' but we may also use the locution for particular purposes – to answer a question, to announce a verdict, to give a warning, etc. In this sense we are performing an illocutionary act. This led Austin and others who followed him to talk of SPEECH ACTS, the classification of utterances in terms of promises, warnings, etc. Paradoxically, towards the end of the book, although he began by contrasting performatives and constatives, Austin (1962: 133) suggests that statements, i.e. constatives, are merely one kind of speech act, for, he argues, to state is 'as much to perform an illocutionary act as, say, to warn or to pronounce'. Nevertheless, linguistically, the notions of performative (in such sentences as *I promise . . .*, etc.) and of speech act (in *There is a bull in the field* as a warning) are very different. Performatives are formally marked and easily identifiable; speech acts are not. We can, in fact, distinguish a number of different kinds of linguistic phenomena which are related but are not quite the same. At one extreme there are the examples with which Austin began. *I name this ship Queen Elizabeth* has two clear characteristics. To begin with, it is part of an action, that of christening a ship; further, it begins with *I* plus a present tense verb, which names the action while performing it. A similar example (in writing, not speech) is *I give and bequeath my watch to my brother*. Slightly different are the utterances that begin *I promise . . ., I warn . . ., I promise to come tomorrow, I warn you that there is a bull in the field*. These are performatives in that they are to be seen as the action of promising, warning, etc., and that the action is named by the verb (and with both *I* and a present tense verb again). But they differ from the first type of performative in that (1) they are not part of any conventional or ritual behaviour, and (2) the performative verb may be omitted without the loss of the illocutionary force; the naming of the action does not seem to be an absolute requirement. We can promise without using the verb *promise*, but we cannot christen a ship without using the verb *name*. Similarly, we may compare *warn* with *bet* as in *I bet you sixpence it will rain tomorrow*. The bet is not 'on' unless the words *I bet . . .* are used. *I bet . . .* then is a performative in the earlier stricter sense, in that the performative verb is an essential element and cannot be omitted. We should also include here expressions with the verb in the passive, but still clearly containing a performative verb. Austin's examples are *You are hereby authorized to pay . . ., Passengers are warned to cross the track by the bridge only, Notice is hereby given that trespassers will be prosecuted*.

At the other extreme, there are utterances such as *There is a bull in the field* which may be a warning or a boast or simply the giving of a piece of information. It is this last type of utterance that has largely interested philosophers. But this type is different from the others and raises problems that they do not. There is no overt indication of the kind of speech act involved. This means that it is very difficult in practice to determine whether a particular utterance is to be characterised as a particular kind of speech act. Even the speaker may not have a clear idea of his own intentions. He may say *There is a bull in the field* because he is a little afraid for his companions, but is that enough to constitute a warning? People's intentions and purposes are often far from clear even to themselves – yet the notion of speech act seems at least to require that we know the use to which the utterance is being put.

Intermediate between these two extremes, there are linguistic devices such as the modal verbs *shall* and *may/can* which are used to make promises and give permission (and *must* to lay obligation). Austin mentions *I shall come tomorrow* as an example of an implicit performative. The status of these is a little problematic. We could argue that, since *You shall have it tomorrow* and *You can go now*, are clearly and unambiguously a promise and granting of permission, *shall* and *can* are essentially performative verbs. But it could also be argued that *You can go now* is more like *There is a bull in the field*, in that it states that it is possible for you to go, but that this is to be understood as deriving from permission by the speaker. The issue is the degree to which these verbs have become conventional markers of promise and permission. There is a more complex problem with *Can you pass the salt?* (discussed in 6.8).

Rather different are more familiar expressions which are performative in the sense that they are essentially part of an action. Examples are the calls in bridge *Three clubs*, *No bid*, etc., or the call in cricket *No ball*. For uttering the bridge call binds the speaker to that contract, while in cricket the umpire's *No ball* makes the delivery a 'no ball' in the sense that the batsman cannot now be out by being bowled, stumped, caught or l.b.w.

Performatives cannot be true or false, but they can 'go wrong' or be 'unhappy' or 'infelicitous'. Saying *I name this ship Queen Elizabeth* will not name the ship if the speaker has no authority to do so. To bet is not merely to say *I bet . . .*, and these words would not be taken as a bet AFTER the relevant race. Searle (1969: 57–61) suggests that speech acts can be characterised in terms of 'felicity conditions' and that there are three kinds of condition that a speech act must meet. First, there are the preparatory conditions. For a promise, these are (roughly) that the hearer would like the action done and that the speaker knows this, but that it is not obvious to either that the speaker will perform the action in the normal course of events. For a request, they are that the hearer can perform the action and that the speaker knows this, and again that it is not obvious to either that the hearer will perform the action in the normal course of events. For an assertion, they are that the speaker has evidence for the truth of what he says and that it is not obvious to either that the hearer knows the facts. Secondly, there are the sincerity conditions: for a promise, that the speaker intends to act; for a request, that he wants the hearer to act; and for an assertion, that he believes what he says. Thirdly, the essential conditions are that the speaker intends that his utterance will 'count as' a promise, etc., and that the hearer should be informed of that intention (this is irrespective of whether he is sincere or not – a promise is still a promise even if I have no intention to act, but an utterance would not be a promise if I did not intend it to be so).

It would be a great step forward if we could unambiguously isolate and characterise speech acts in this way. In practice, it is virtually impossible to determine just how many speech acts are required. One possibility is that we might determine them in terms of a limited set of possible felicity conditions, but, in fact, it seems more likely that we shall be able to establish the felicity conditions only after we have determined what are the speech acts. Alternatively, we might determine them in terms of the actual performative verbs that occur. Thus we recognise warnings and promises as speech acts because we have the verbs *warn* and *promise*, and Austin suggested that the number of performative verbs was in the order of four figures (the 'third power of ten' he said). But there is no obvious reason for believing that every speech act recognised by the linguist must have a corresponding verb in the language. Another possibility is that we could determine the speech acts from the verbs that are used for reporting them – *He said that . . ., He promised that . . .* But there is a similar problem here too. The layman admittedly can only report as speech acts those for which he has an appropriate verb, but it does not seem to follow that the linguist or philosopher should recognise as speech acts only those that the language allows the layman to report. We must surely doubt whether the existence of a list of verbs in a dictionary can provide the list of possible types of speech acts. Moreover, speech acts are probably independent of the actual language, at least to some degree. Would we recognise different speech acts for French and English if the list of verbs was different in each?

It would be no less difficult to determine unambiguously what is the speech act being performed in each utterance. The main difficulty here is that there seems to be no very direct relation between speech act and the form of the words used. We cannot identify speech act with sentence type, as we have already seen (6.8), but further we cannot even identify speech acts with sentences containing performative verbs. A sentence beginning *I promise* could be a warning, while one can make a tentative judgment with *I bet* (*I bet he won't come*).

7.4 *Presupposition*

Philosophers have been concerned for some time with the status of sentences such as *The King of France is bald*. The question is whether, if there is, in fact, no King of France, such a sentence can be said to be false.

On one view, originally suggested by Russell (1905), this sentence ASSERTS both that there is a King of France and that he is bald, and, therefore, if there is no King of France, the sentence must be false.

There is an alternative solution, associated with Strawson (1964), which says that, in using expressions like the King of France (REFERRING EXPRESSIONS), the speaker assumes that the hearer can identify the person or thing being spoken about. He does not, therefore, assert that the person or thing exists, but merely PRESUPPOSES his or its existence. If the person or thing does not exist there is 'presupposition failure' and the sentence is not false; it is neither true nor false, and there is a 'truth-value gap'. The same judgment, moreover, is made about the negative sentence *The King of France isn't bald*. This, too, has no truth value (but on the first view it would be true, since it would deny the false statement that the King of France exists).

There is a similar suggestion with what have been called 'factive predicates', which are associated with such words as *significant* and *regret*. The sentences *It is significant that John came early* and *I regret that she spoke* presuppose that John came early and that she spoke. By contrast, there are no such presuppositions for similar sentences with 'non-factive' *likely* and *believe* – *It is likely that John came early, I believe that she spoke*.

It has been further claimed that presupposition can be defined logically, in that presuppositions are 'constant under negation' (Kiparsky & Kiparsky 1971: 351): they are logically implied by both a positive sentence and its negative counterpart. Thus *It isn't significant that John came early* and *I don't regret that she spoke* have the same presuppositions as the positive sentences, and we have already seen that both *The King of France is bald* and *The King of France isn't bald* are said to presuppose that there is a King of France.

Most obviously this kind of presupposition holds for various types of noun phrase such as the referring expressions or the factive predicates. Similarly, *John married/didn't marry Fred's sister* presupposes that Fred had a sister, and *John was/wasn't worried by his wife's infidelity* presupposes that his wife was unfaithful.

There is, however, one serious problem with the negation test. It is possible to negate the sentence in order to deny the presupposition. Although *John wasn't worried by his wife's infidelity* is usually taken to presuppose that his wife was unfaithful, it could be used to suggest that she was not unfaithful, as is shown by the extended sentence *John wasn't worried by his wife's infidelity, because she had not in fact been unfaithful*. Exactly the same considerations hold for all the other negative sentences that we have been considering. There is nothing odd about *It isn't significant that John came early, because he didn't*, *The King of France isn't bald – there is no King of France*, *I don't regret that she spoke, because she didn't* (cf. Kempson 1975: 66–70, 85–7).

This problem of negation does not arise with the other view of presupposition. This maintains, quite simply, that *The King of France is bald* asserts both that there is a King of France and that he is bald. If either of these two assertions is false, then the whole sentence must be false. This, moreover, can be dealt with logically in terms of the logic of 'and' (see 8.3). Similar considerations hold for *I regret that she spoke* and *John was worried by his wife's infidelity*; both equally make two assertions and either may be false. This seems to be supported by our language. For in reply to *John was worried by his wife's infidelity*, it is possible to say *That's not true: she wasn't unfaithful* as well as *That's not true: he wasn't a bit worried by it*. These replies seem to assume that two assertions are being made, and that either of them can be false and so falsify the whole sentence.

This, however, seems contrary to our intuitions. We should normally interpret *John wasn't worried by his wife's infidelity* as meaning that he wasn't worried and not that she wasn't unfaithful. The interpretation that she wasn't unfaithful can only be achieved if we extend with, e.g., *because she wasn't unfaithful*. It seems reasonable to say, with the second view of presupposition, that it is the assertion not the presupposition that is normally denied by negation, and that denial of the presupposition is unusual and 'marked'. Moreover, it is clear that the two potential assertions do not have the same status. That there is a King of France may be true or false independently of any assertion about baldness, but the assertion about baldness is intelligible only if we know who it is that is said to be bald, and though it may be true or false, it can only be true or false, it would seem, if the other assertion is true (that there is a King of France). This, of course, is precisely what the presuppositional view claims – that there is 'presupposition failure', and it is difficult to see how it can be rejected.

Both solutions, however, face a difficulty in the fact that presuppositions appear to be constant, not only under negation, but also under question. Thus *Is the King of France bald?* and *Was John worried by his wife's infidelity?* presuppose that there is a King of France and that John's wife was unfaithful. But both solutions to the problem are based on assumptions about an assertion (or denial) about baldness or about John's being worried, and questions, of course, make no assertion at all. The same presuppositions hold for the negative questions *Isn't the King of France bald?* and *Wasn't John worried by his wife's infidelity?* They also hold, moreover, for suggestions, commands, invitations, e.g. *Let's visit the King of France* or *Don't talk to John about his wife's infidelity*.

Strawson also points out (1964 [1971: 95–6]) that, although *The King of France is bald* may be neither true nor false, we might reasonably argue that *The exhibition was visited yesterday by the King of France* is false if there is no King of France, for, whoever the exhibition was visited by, it was not visited by the King of France. The essential issue here appears to be that of topic and comment (7.2), for *The King of France is bald* can be taken either as saying of the King of France (the topic) that he is bald (the comment), or of saying about bald people (the topic) that they include the King of France. On the first interpretation, where the King of France is the topic, it would seem more reasonable to talk about truth-value gap: the King of France can hardly be said to be bald if he does not exist. On the second, it would seem equally reasonable to say that the sentence is false: bald people do not include the King of France, if there is no King of France. Similar considerations would hold for *John was worried by his wife's infidelity*. This seems to be neither true nor false as a reply to *What was his reaction to his wife's infidelity?* (if she was not unfaithful) and, indeed, the question is inappropriate; but it could reasonably be regarded as false as a reply to *What was John worried by?*

The examples we have been considering have all contained referring expressions or factive predicates. These have in common the fact that they are grammatically noun phrases which in some sense indicate the 'existence' of what is being referred to, in either a physical or a factual sense – the King of France, the fact that John's wife was unfaithful. But we can also extend presupposition to, e.g., *Fred continued/didn't continue speaking*, where it is presupposed that he was speaking previously (Keenan 1971: 47). Similarly, the notorious *When did you stop beating your wife?* presupposes that you once beat her. The first example illustrates again that a presupposition may be constant under negation, but the second that it is also involved with questions. This kind of presupposition is not very different from that of the factive predicates – we can generalise about 'aspectual' verbs such as *continue*, *stop*, *resume*, *quit*. There is also clearly presuppositional meaning associated with *other* and *again*. *Bill drank another glass of beer* presupposes that he had drunk at least one. It may be remembered that when the Mad Hatter invited Alice to 'take some more tea', she declined, saying that she couldn't have any more as she hadn't had any yet.

Rather different is the suggestion that presupposition is associated with specific features of certain lexical items. Thus it has been said that *I cleaned/didn't clean the room* presupposes that the room was dirty, and that *I killed/didn't kill the bird* presupposes that the bird was alive. This, then, involves the presuppositions of the verbs *clean* and *kill*. But there is danger here that we shall have to treat the multitude of semantic features that are associated with collocation or 'selectional restrictions' as matters of presupposition. *Hear*, presumably, presupposes that its object is audible; this will account for the unacceptability of **I heard the cloud*. But this seems not very different from the unacceptability of **I killed* *the cloud* (or even **I cleaned the cloud*). Slightly differently, it has been said that *John is a bachelor* presupposes that John is a man, but asserts that he is unmarried, since *John isn't a bachelor* would normally be taken to give the information that he is married, not that he is a female. It is certainly true that 'unmarried' seems to be the more significant part of the meaning of *bachelor*, but this is almost certainly a matter of the relations between the available lexical terms. To indicate that John is male we have the term *man* available, and *woman* for 'female', and these terms say nothing about marital status. To indicate marital status we have only the terms *bachelor* and *spinster*, which also indicate sex; but the fact that we also have *man* and *woman* means that they are not needed for sex reference, and that is why they are used primarily to indicate marital status.

More subtly, Fillmore (1971b: 282) has suggested that *accuse* presupposes that the act referred to was bad, but states that a certain person did it, while *criticise* presupposes that someone did it, but states that it was bad. But these verbs are reports of speech acts and they indicate that it is the subject (e.g. *John* in *John accused* . . ., *John criticised* . . .) who assumes that the action was bad and says that the person committed it, or assumes that the person did it and says that it was bad. But this is not presupposition in the sense in which we have been considering it. For it was the SPEAKER who made the presuppositions (and assumed that the hearer made the same ones). Here we have reports of what the SUBJECT of sentences assumes and says. If there is presupposition and assertion, it is the presupposition and assertion of the subject of the sentence, being reported by the speaker (who may not necessarily share the same beliefs).

If we use presupposition quite loosely to include anything that it is reasonable to believe the speaker is assuming or taking for granted, the term can be extended in many ways. For instance, Lakoff (1971b: 333; 1971c: 63) says of the sentence *John told Mary that she was ugly and then shé insulted him* that this presupposes that telling someone she is ugly is to insult her. But, of course, this results only because the stress pattern is typically used where it is stated that the action is repeated with the subject and object reversed, as in *John hit Mary and then shé hit hím*. Nevertheless, the fact that the speaker has used this intonation shows that he assumes that saying a woman is ugly is to insult her. On the other hand, we do not treat this in ordinary language as part of the propositional content of the sentence, either asserted or presupposed. For, in contrast with what we noted earlier, it would not be normal to reply *That's not true, saying someone is ugly is not to insult*.

An even broader view of presupposition is that of Fillmore (1971b: 275–6) who first discusses the felicity conditions (see 7.3) for a sentence such as *Please shut the door* – including the relationship between speaker and hearer, the hearer's ability to shut the door, the fact that the door is open and the fact that the speaker wants it closed. Yet none of these would seem to be obviously describable in terms of propositions which the speaker believes. In a similar sort of way, Keenan (1971: 51) suggests that French *Tu es dégoûtant* presupposes that the hearer is inferior to, or intimate with, the speaker (see 3.5); but he treats this as PRAGMATIC presupposition, as opposed to the LOGICAL presupposition of referring expressions, factive predicates, etc.

The range of discussion shows that we have two major problems, neither of them easily solved. The first is whether we can draw a distinction between what is asserted and what is presupposed. In spite of Russell's claim, it is reasonable to argue that we can and that we should, even though there are difficulties. The second is what phenomena should be brought under the heading of presupposition. This is far more difficult, since the phenomena are disparate, but not unrelated. It would be sensible to exclude what are obviously contextual felicity conditions, partly at least because they are not, or not easily, describable in propositional terms. For the rest it is, perhaps, reasonable to restrict the notion of presupposition either to what is assumed to be true (so that in certain circumstances at least the negation test will operate), or to assumptions about 'existence' in the wide sense of the term.

7.5 *Implicatures*

In the last section one suggestion was that we should attempt to restrict *presupposition* to propositions or information that is assumed by the speaker (and assumed by him to be known to the hearer). But the speaker may use similar devices to imply further information that the hearer does not know. He may imply what he does not actually say. Thus, *It's cold in here* might be taken as a request to close a window. (Here the term *imply* is used in an ordinary non-logical sense, and *say* to refer to sentence meaning.)

An attempt to account for this was made by Grice (1975) in terms of the notion of implicature. Grice suggests that there is a general CO-OPERATIVE PRINCIPLE between speaker and hearer, which, roughly, controls the way in which a conversation may proceed. He then distinguishes four categories under each of which there are several MAXIMS. These are:

Quantity
      (1) Make your contribution as informative as required (for the current purpose of the exchange).
      (2) Do not make your contribution more informative than is required.

Quality   Try to make your contribution one that is true.
      (1) Do not say what you believe to be false.
      (2) Do not say that for which you lack evidence.

Relation   Be relevant.

Manner   Be perspicuous.
      (1) Avoid obscurity of expression.
      (2) Avoid ambiguity.
      (3) Be brief.
      (4) Be orderly.

The maxim of quantity can be used to account for the fact that, if someone says *Have you finished your homework and put your books away?* and the reply is *I have finished my homework*, the questioner can infer that the books have not been put away. For, if the replier is not violating the maxim of quantity, he would have given the information that he had put the books away, perhaps by a simple *Yes*, if he had done so. Similarly, *It may be raining* implies that the speaker does not know whether it is, for, if he did, he would have said *It is raining*, which is more informative than *It may be raining*. (For a more detailed exposition, see Lyons 1977: 594–5.) One very important point to note here, though it is often ignored, is the relevance of intonation. The use of the fall-rise, for instance, is largely associated with the maxim of quantity, for it says 'but . . .' or 'that is all I can say – draw your own conclusions'. It would, therefore, be an appropriate tune for either of our examples – *I have finished my ˇhomework, It ˇmay be raining*. In other cases, it may not be obvious from the context precisely what it is the speaker is not saying, as in *He is very ˇclever*, but the tune warns the hearer that he must work this out. The maxim of relation can often be invoked too. Grice (1975: 51) has the example *There is a garage round the corner* as a reply to *I am out of petrol*. This implicates that the garage is probably open; otherwise, the comment would not be relevant.

The chief interest in implicatures, however, has centred on the occasions when they derive, not from the observation of the maxims, but from their violation. Grice's best known example is of a reference for a job in philosophy that reads *Dear Sir, Mr X's command of English is excellent and his attendance at tutorials has been regular. Yours, etc.* Since the writer knows that more information than this is required, he is clearly flouting the maxim of quantity. He is presumably wishing to convey information that he does not wish to write down, i.e. that Mr X is no good at philosophy. The maxim of quality, Grice argues, is flouted by irony (*John's a fine friend*) and metaphor (*You're the cream in my coffee*) – and the hearer has to work out what it is that the speaker is trying to convey.

In the examples we have been considering, the implicature

depends, in part, on the context and the beliefs of the speaker and hearer. But Grice also notes that there are some implicatures that depend solely on the conventional meaning of the words. Thus, *He is an Englishman: he is, therefore, brave* implicates that it follows from his being an Englishman that he is brave, although we shall not want to claim that it actually says that. This kind of implicature Grice refers to as CONVENTIONAL implicature as contrasted with the previous CONVERSATIONAL implicature. But the distinction is not always clear: examples of metaphor, for instance, often seem more 'conventional' than 'conversational'.

The conversational implicatures that derive from the maxim of quantity have the characteristic that they may be cancelled. Thus, *I tried to phone John yesterday* would normally implicate that I did not in fact phone him, but there is nothing odd about continuing . . . *and in fact I succeeded in getting through*. Similarly, *Most languages have at least one sibilant* implicates that some languages have none, but we can equally say *Most, if not all, languages have at least one sibilant* (Lyons 1977: 595–6).

The notion of implicatures can handle all the cases dealt with under presupposition. *The King of France is bald* implicates that there is a King of France according to the maxims of relevance and, perhaps, quantity, for one would not talk about the King of France if there were not one. But it would be unfortunate if this suggested that we can draw no line between what is presupposed and what is implicated, for the latter alone assumes that the speaker actually intends to provide information that is not part of his sentence meaning.

Moreover, it is difficult to see how Grice's suggestions could actually be put into practice for a description of meaning. For they are too vague. The maxim of relation, for instance, tells us nothing about what it means for an utterance to be relevant, and Grice himself saw this as a serious problem. A recent suggestion is that we can define an utterance as relevant if, taken together with another utterance, it yields new information that is not derivable from each utterance alone, and that the maxim of relation is the only one we need (Smith & Wilson 1979: 177). But this takes us no further, for we should still want to know how to define precisely what are the conditions for the provision of this new information (see 8.6).

8

SEMANTICS AND LOGIC

We have already briefly discussed the possible relevance of logic to the linguistic study of semantics (1.4, 5.1). There will be an attempt here to deal briefly, and as simply as possible, with a few basic concepts of logic, and to see their application to some linguistic problems. (For an excellent introduction see Allwood, Andersson & Dähl 1977.)

8.1 Logic and language

The terms *logic* and *logical* are often used simply to mean 'reasonable' or 'sensible'. But there is a stricter sense of the terms to refer to formal logical systems which have much in common with mathematical systems, and which deal with the validity of inferences.

A favourite example from traditional logic textbooks is:

All men are mortal.
Socrates is a man.
Therefore Socrates is mortal.

Here the CONCLUSION (the third sentence) follows from the PREMISES (the first two sentences). The INFERENCE is LOGICALLY valid. Notice, however, that this would not be true of:

All men are mortal.
Socrates is a mortal.
Therefore Socrates is a man.

A moment's reflection will show that here there is a false conclusion, for *Socrates* might be the name of my cat.

We often reach conclusions along such lines without actually stating all the premises. For instance, we might conclude that Maurice is fabulously rich because we know that he is a pop-star; here the premises are *All pop-stars are fabulously rich* and *Maurice is a pop-star*. We cannot, however, conclude that Maurice is a pop-star because we know that he is fabulously rich, using the same premises. That conclusion would require the premise *All fabulously rich people are pop-stars*, which is untrue. Yet such false conclusions are often arrived at, especially in areas such as politics. Similarly, we may reason as follows:

> *John is either at home or in his office.*
> *John is not at home.*
> *Therefore John is in his office.*

If the premises are true, the conclusion follows: it also is true.

To capture the properties of sentences which make valid conclusions such as those we have been considering, logicians are concerned with the LOGICAL FORM of such sentences, and this can be shown (as we have already seen) by the use of a formal language, using specialised symbols whose status is exactly the same as those of mathematics. Thus, the example about John being at home can be symbolised $((p \vee q)\ \&\sim p) \rightarrow q$, which is no more mysterious than symbolising the statement that if you add two apples to four and remove half you will have three by $(4 + 2) \div 2 = 3$.

It is important to realise that the conventions of any particular language or the actual state of the world in no way affect the validity of traditional logic. Thus, our conclusion about Socrates does not depend upon the meaning of the words *men* or *mortal* (though it does depend, of course, upon the logical structure, which is in part represented by the grammatical structure and such words as *all* – see 8.3). Where there are correspondences between logical symbols and words of the language they are not always exact. Thus $\exists$ may be translated 'some' but, unlike *some*, includes 'one' as well as 'more than one' and, also unlike *some*, has no implication of 'not all'; for *Some men are mortal* is held to be true if *All men are mortal* is true. Similarly, $\vee$ may be glossed 'or', but does not indicate a choice between two alternatives; it means rather 'either one or the other or both' (but see below on exclusive and inclusive *or*). Logic does not even depend for its validity on any intuitions we may have about its correctness. Thus, it can be shown, by material implication (8.2), that *If I am invisible, everyone can see me* is perfectly valid if interpreted logically. But equally, of course, our intuitions are often at variance with mathematical concepts, such as those concerned with infinity, e.g. that parallel lines meet in infinity. Nor would the argument be invalid if there were no men, or if, in fact, they were not mortal, or if Socrates were not, in fact, a man. Thus, for instance, *All men are immortal. Socrates is a man. Therefore Socrates is immortal* is a valid argument.

Yet there would be little interest in this if it could not be applied to language. The issue is not whether language is or is not 'logical' (it is not), but how far the application of logic will serve to explain some linguistic phenomena. We shall see in the following pages how logic can deal with problems and ambiguities that grammar fails to solve. For instance, *I'm looking for a pencil* is ambiguous as shown by the continuations *and when I find it . . .* or *and when I find one . . .*. Again, linguists have found difficulty with the fact that *Everybody in this room speaks two languages* seems to have a different meaning from *Two languages are spoken by everybody in this room* (Katz & Postal 1964: 72). A very familiar and very old joke is one that can be played with *no one, nobody*, etc., as when Odysseus in Homer's *Odyssey* told the giant Polyphemus that his name was 'No one' and Polyphemus' friends would not come to his aid when he said no one had hurt him. Typically the joke appears also in Lewis Carroll: 'Who did you pass on the road?' . . . 'Nobody' . . . 'Quite right, this young lady saw him too. So of course Nobody walks slower than you.' All these can be, and have been, explained in simple logical terms.

8.2 *Propositional logic*

Although the term PROPOSITIONAL LOGIC is used here (and widely elsewhere), alternative names are PROPOSITIONAL CALCULUS and SENTENTIAL CALCULUS. In view of the problems concerned with propositions, the last is, perhaps, preferable; certainly we shall be talking in this section about sentences, not propositions.

We are here concerned with the relations that hold between sentences, especially relations involving complex sentences, irrespective of the internal structure of the sentences themselves. Thus, in an example in 8.1, we have the two sentences *John is in his office* and *John is at home* and the information that (at least) one of these is true. Given that the second is false, we can conclude that the first is true. This conclusion can be drawn irrespective of the form of the sentences themselves. Thus from *Either John is in his office or whales are fishes*, we can draw the conclusion *John is in his office* if *whales are fishes* is false. (The fact that it is unlikely that we should ever say this is irrelevant to the logical analysis.) Instead, therefore, of using actual sentences we may use symbols such as p, q, and r (SENTENTIAL VARIABLES) to represent the sentences. We also need symbols for the LOGICAL CONNECTIVES:

$\sim$	negation	('not')
&	conjunction	('and')
v	disjunction	(inclusive 'or')
$\rightarrow$	implication	('if . . . then')
$\equiv$	equivalence	('if and only if . . . then')

We can now symbolise not only 'p and q', 'p or q', etc. (as p & q, p v q), but quite complex sentences. The inference above can be represented as $((p \vee q) \mathbin{\&} \sim q) \rightarrow p$ which says, 'if p-or-q and not-q, then p'. The brackets here are important to show the structure, for obviously 'p-or-q and not-q' is different from 'p or q-and-not-q', which would have to be shown as p v $(q \mathbin{\&} \sim q)$. There is a similar ambiguity in *John and Bill or*

Fred. (There are rules that would allow us to dispense with some of these brackets, but the formulae are easier to read with them in.) It becomes apparent from this that we need RULES OF FORMATION to form these more compound sentences, and that the logical connectives do not hold only between the simple sentences *p*, *q*, etc., but also between the compound sentences. This is all part of the LOGICAL SYNTAX.

We also need to define the connectives (and this is dealt with under LOGICAL SEMANTICS). It will be remembered that we were concerned with the truth or falsity of our simple sentences, and, indeed, with the truth and falsity of compound sentences in relation to the truth and falsity of the simple sentences of which they are formed. It is assumed here that every sentence is either true or false – that it can be assigned the TRUTH VALUE 'true' or 'false', symbolised **t** and **f**. Given the truth value of the simple sentences, we can deduce the truth value of any compound sentence provided we know the 'meaning' of the connectives.

It now becomes possible to set up TRUTH TABLES for each of the connectives. These indicate what is the truth value of the compound sentence in relation to the truth value of the simple sentence from which it is formed. For & ('and'), for instance, the compound sentences will be true only if the simple sentences are true. We can, therefore, set up the truth table for conjunction (&) as:

p	*q*	*p* & *q*
t	t	t
t	f	f
f	t	f
f	f	f

The first line shows that, if both simple sentences *p* and *q* are true, the compound sentence is true; the next three lines show that, if either *p* or *q* or both are false, the compound sentence is false. This is, very largely, in accordance with the normal use of *and*. It could, however, be argued that in ordinary language we might say that the compound sentence

was only half-true or that only half of it was true in the second
and third cases. For the logician, however, conjunction involves the truth values shown in the table.

For negation the truth table is simply:

p	$\sim p$
t	f
f	t

Here we need only one sentence p, together with its negation
$\sim p$. This, of course, says that, if a sentence is not true, it is
false, and vice versa. But again in ordinary language we do
not always accept this. If asked whether it is raining or not,
we might well say *It's doing neither the one thing nor the other*.
There are also problems with antonyms and complementaries. It will be remembered, for instance, that *John isn't
honest* would usually mean that John is dishonest, whereas
John isn't clever would not suggest that he is stupid (5.4).

The truth table for disjunction is:

p	q	$p \lor q$
t	t	t
t	f	t
f	t	t
f	f	f

This is related to *or* except that the first line allows for the
compound to be true if both simple sentences are true. In
ordinary language *either . . . or . . .* usually means that only
one of the sentences is true. Thus we might argue:

John is either at home or in his office.
John is at home.
Therefore he is not in his office.

This involves EXCLUSIVE *or*, but logical disjunction is concerned with INCLUSIVE *or*, which allows not only that either
sentence may be true, but also that both sentences may be
true. Ordinary language sometimes permits inclusive *or*. For
instance, a regulation might apply to 'anyone who is female

or over 65'. But this would not apply only to women under 65 and men over 65; it would also include women over 65, who are both female and over 65. In a logical formula exclusive *or* has to be stated by $(p \lor q) \& \sim (p \& q)$; it adds, that is to say, to inclusive '*p* or *q*' the condition 'not both *p* and *q*'.

Although implication is related to *if . . . then*, there is one striking difference. In ordinary language we normally relate sentences with *if . . . then* only if there is some causal (or similar) relationship between them. But this would not be permissible in propositional logic, because it takes no account of the nature of the sentences themselves. As with conjunction and disjunction, we need a connective that will simply relate (ANY) sentences in terms of their truth values. The truth table for implication is, in fact:

p	q	$p \rightarrow q$
t	t	t
t	f	f
f	t	t
f	f	t

According to this any true statement will imply any other true statement. Therefore we can infer:

If the horse is a mammal, the shark is a fish.

But a false sentence is shown in the table as implying both false and true sentences. We can thus infer:

If the horse is a bird, the shark is a mammal.
If the horse is a bird, the shark is a fish.

(If *The horse is a bird* is false, both the false *The shark is a mammal* and the true *The shark is a fish* can be inferred.) More strikingly we can infer (if *I am invisible* is false):

If I am invisible, no one can see me.
If I am invisible, everyone can see me.

Although this may seem quite absurd, it has some correlation with usage in language:

If he's president, I'm a Dutchman/I'll eat my hat.

Here one false sentence implies another false sentence.

The essential point, however, is clear. Implication in the logical sense, like any of the connectives, does not necessarily correspond exactly to the use of anything found in natural language. It owes its validity solely to the truth functions assigned to it. (This is, however, MATERIAL IMPLICATION. For STRICT IMPLICATION see 8.6.)

Finally, equivalence is simply the conjunction of two implications: $p \equiv q$ equals $(p \rightarrow q)$ & $(q \rightarrow p)$. It is usually expressed in ordinary language as *only if* (though as with implication there is usually some causal connection between the two sentences in ordinary language). The truth table is:

p	q	$p \equiv q$
t	t	t
t	f	f
f	t	f
f	f	t

It is worth noting briefly that we can, in fact, operate with only two of the connectives we have mentioned, negation and conjunction. For $p \rightarrow q \equiv \sim p \vee q \equiv \sim(p \mathbin{\&} \sim q)$. These can be checked by truth tables or intuitively, e.g. by the equivalence of *If John stays, I leave* and *Either John doesn't stay or I leave* $((p \rightarrow q) \equiv (\sim p \vee q))$.

Given the meaning of the connectives we can work out the truth value of quite complex compound sentences from simple sentences. But of special interest are compound sentences that are true irrespective of whether the initial sentences are true or false, their truth depending on the connectives alone. These are called TAUTOLOGIES. One such is $p \vee \sim p$, for this will be true whether p is true or false. Other fairly obvious ones are $(p \mathbin{\&} q) \rightarrow p$, and (since $p \mathbin{\&} q$ is false if p is false) $\sim p \rightarrow \sim (p \mathbin{\&} q)$. More complex is the formula for handling the conclusion in 8.1 about John being in his office – $((p \vee q) \mathbin{\&} \sim q) \rightarrow p$, for it can be worked out from the truth table that this is always true irrespective of the truth of *p* and *q*. It is because this is a tautology that we know that our conclusion is correct.

Propositional logic has been of relevance once in our previous discussion. It will be recalled that one solution to the problem of *The King of France is bald* is that it asserts both that there is a King of France and that he is bald. Its logical structure would be, then, *p & q*. Now if it is the case that the negation test does not work, because we may say either *The King of France isn't bald – he has plenty of hair* or *The King of France isn't bald – there is no King of France*, we can account for this by the simple fact that *p & q* is false if either *p* or *q* is false. *The King of France is bald* does not, in the analysis, presuppose that there is a King of France. It implies it (logically) since $(p \& q) \rightarrow p$. If there is no King of France or if he is not bald, the whole sentence is false, since $\sim p \rightarrow \sim (p \& q)$ and $\sim q \rightarrow \sim (p \& q)$. One virtue of this approach, it is claimed, is that it can handle the whole problem in terms of a two-value logic involving only 'true' and 'false', whereas the presuppositional account involves a third truth value 'neither true nor false' (when there is presupposition failure and a truth-value gap).

We saw that there is some support for this view in ordinary language in that we can say *That's not true – there is no King of France*. But this is far from a typical response. Moreover, it is not even the case that in ordinary language we always accept $\sim p \rightarrow \sim (p \& q)$ – that, if one sentence in a conjoined pair of sentences is untrue, the WHOLE complex sentence is untrue. If I say *John is very rich and lives in the Bahamas*, when in fact he lives in Bermuda, we might not wish to say that what I said was untrue, but only that it was half true or that only part of it was true. The fact that we CAN handle the problem in logical terms does not necessarily show that we SHOULD, and the points already made show that a logical analysis does not accord well with our intuitions or with linguistic practice. Moreover, most of the arguments presented in 7.4 suggest very strongly that such an analysis is likely to be unsatisfactory. The point, quite simply, is that we should attempt a logical analysis only if we have first shown that the analysis in terms of assertion is correct. We cannot, or should not, use the fact that we can deal with the problem in logical terms as an argument in favour of such an analysis.

8.3 *Predicate logic*

Since propositional logic deals solely with relations between sentences, it cannot account for inference that depends upon relations within sentences. It cannot, for instance, deal with our example:

> *All men are mortal.*
> *Socrates is a man.*
> *Therefore Socrates is mortal.*

For this we need PREDICATE LOGIC or PREDICATE CALCULUS, but since in predicate logic we shall need to deal also with relations between sentences, predicate logic is not wholly distinct from propositional logic, but includes it.

There was a preliminary account of the notions of predicate logic in 5.1 and 6.6. We discussed individual constants a, b, c, individual variables x, y, z and predicates F, G, H, etc. The universal quantifier ∀ was also introduced, and it was mentioned that we are concerned in logic only with sentences, not with open sentences such as $W(x)$. We need to convert such an open sentence either by substituting individual constants – $W(a)$, or by introducing a quantifier – $\forall x(W(x))$. We can, moreover, symbolise *All men are mortal* as $\forall x(M(x) \rightarrow D(x))$, where M stands for 'man' and D for 'mortal' ('For all xs, if x is a man, x is mortal').

A second quantifier is the existential quantifier ∃, which expresses 'some' or, more strictly, means 'there is at least one individual for whom it is the case that. . .' *Some men are foolish* is then symbolised:

$\exists x(M(x) \ \& \ F(x))$

This can be read 'there are some xs that are both men and

foolish'. Notice that the sentence connectives are different. If we had written & instead of → with the ∀ example, this would have said (incorrectly) that every individual is both man and mortal, while → instead of & with the ∃ example would not say that there were some men who were foolish, but that there are some individuals (or at least one) who would be foolish if they were men.

We can now symbolise our Socrates example:

$$\forall x(M(x) \rightarrow D(x))$$
$$M(a)$$
$$\therefore D(a)$$

We cannot, however, infer that, if Socrates is a mortal, he is a man (he might be my cat). Nor could we make the inference if the first premise had been *Some men are mortal*. The following are, therefore, incorrect inferences:

(1) $\forall x(M(x) \rightarrow D(x))$
    $D(x)$
  $\therefore M(x)$

(2) $\exists x(M(x) \And D(x))$
    $M(x)$
  $\therefore D(x)$

It is easy to see why these inferences hold in terms of simple set theory. In Figure 8 the larger circle represents the set of individuals who are mortal (D), and the middle circle the set of individuals who are men (M), and this is inside the larger circle. It follows from this that any individual in the M

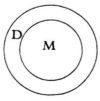

Figure 8

set, such as Socrates, is also in the D set, but not, of course, that any individual in the D set is in the M set (he may or may not be).

With the existential quantifier all we know is that the sets of mortals and men intersect – that there is at least one who is in both sets, both mortal and a man (Figure 9). From this, of course, it does not follow that any individual in one set is also in the other, but at least one must be.

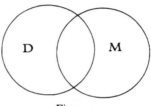

Figure 9

It is worth noting finally that $\forall$ and $\exists$ are logically related to each other in terms of negation. For *All men are mortal* can be paraphrased 'There is no man who is not mortal'. This can be shown by the logical equivalence of:

$$\forall x(M(x) \rightarrow D(x)) \equiv \sim\exists x(M(x) \,\&\, \sim D(x))$$

In a simplified form we have the equivalences:

$$\exists x\,(F(x)) \equiv \sim\forall x\,(\sim F(x))$$
$$\sim\exists x\,(F(x)) \equiv \forall x\,(\sim F(x))$$
$$\exists x\,(\sim F(x)) \equiv \sim\forall x\,(F(x))$$
$$\sim\exists x\,(\sim F(x)) \equiv \forall x\,(F(x))$$

The validity of this can easily be checked. Thus the third says that, if there is something that is not F, it is not the case that everything is F, and vice versa. The rather forbidding symbolisation states some very simple observations.

We can deal with the problem of *nobody*. *Nobody came* has the logical structure $\sim\exists x\,(C(x))$ 'There is no x such that x came', but grammatically it looks like *John came* or *The men came*, which are simply C(a) and $\forall x\, (M(x) \rightarrow C(x))$. The joke arises from the mismatch of grammar and logic.

We noted in 8.2 that there is an ambiguity in *John and Bill or Fred* that can be easily handled with round brackets – (a & b) ∨ c vs. a & (b ∨ c). The round brackets in the first example show that only a and b are linked by & but a and b (together) and c are linked by ∨. This is a matter of SCOPE, and we shall say that & here is 'under the scope of ∨', for it is included in that part of the formula that is affected by ∨ (but not vice versa). In the case of the quantifiers we have assumed (though not actually stated) that what is under their scope is what immediately follows in round brackets. Thus M(x) → D(x) is under the scope of ∀ in $\forall x\, (M(x) \rightarrow D(x))$. This is not the same as ($\forall x\, (M(x)) \rightarrow D(x)$), where only M($x$) is under the scope of ∀, and D(x) is an open sentence which expresses no proposition (it does not tell us what individual or individuals are mortal). The same is true of negation, except that brackets are unnecessary if its scope is the immediately following constituent, e.g. ~p or ~∃x, but we need brackets in ~(p & q) to distinguish it from ~p & q.

There may, however, be more than one quantifier in a sentence and the scope of the quantifier becomes important. For instance, *Everyone loves someone* is ambiguous, since it may mean either that there is a particular person that everyone loves (so that everyone loves the same person) or that each person loves someone (who may, or may not, be a different person in each case). This is dealt with quite simply by writing the quantifiers in a different order, the convention being that the first quantifier has the next one under its scope. We can symbolise then $\exists y\, \forall x (L(x, y))$ and $\forall x\, \exists y (L(x, y))$ which say respectively 'There is a y such that, for all xs, x loves y' and 'For all xs, there is a y such that x loves y'.

Ordinary language does not mark scope consistently with words such as *all*, *some* or the negatives. For, although *Someone did not come* is likely to be interpreted as $\exists x\, (\sim C(x))$, *Everyone didn't come* is more likely to be ~ $\forall x (C(x))$ 'Not every one came', rather than $\forall x\, (\sim C(x))$ 'Everyone failed to come'; and, as we have seen, *Everyone loves someone* is simply ambiguous. But it is the relation between scope and word order that accounts for the problem of *Everyone in this room speaks two languages* and *Two languages are spoken by everyone in this room*. The problem here is that, in general, active and passive sentences seem to have the same meaning. But the most likely interpretation in the first of these sentences is that the pair of languages may be different for the different people, but in the second that they are the same pair (though stress may affect the interpretation). This can be accounted for by the fact that passivisation changes the order of the quantifiers *everyone* and *two* ('a pair') and, therefore, their scope. The logical structures are $\forall x \; \exists y \; (S(x,y))$ and $\exists y \; \forall x \; (S(x,y))$ where x refers to *people in this room*, y to *two languages* and S to *speak*. The same is true of other logical words such as *many*, *few*, which cannot easily be handled in logical terms. Thus *Many men read few books* would normally be taken to mean that many men do very little reading, while *Few books are read by many men* would be taken to mean that there are only a few books that are read by a lot of people (Lakoff 1971a: 238). The difference is easily explained in terms of the scope of *many* and *few*. The scope of *many* and the negative is involved in another pair of sentences (Jackendoff 1969: 222–8): *Many arrows didn't hit the target*, *The target was not hit by many arrows*. On the most likely interpretation, the first says that many arrows actually missed the target, while the second says only that not-many (only a few) hit it (and it could be that none at all actually missed).

8.4 *Intension and extension*

Logical truth, as discussed in the last two sections, is quite independent of the world. It is fairly obvious, therefore, that we need somehow to extend the logical framework to relate it to the world of experience.

Let us begin by noting the distinction made between INTENSIONS and EXTENSIONS (or between INTENSIONAL and EXTENSIONAL meaning). Informally, we may say the extension of an expression is the set of entities which that expression denotes, while its intension is whatever it is that defines that set. Thus, the extension of *cow* is the set of all the cows in the world, but its intension is the property that is described as *bovine*.

Knowing the meaning of an expression, however, cannot be equivalent to knowing its extension, for this would mean that we could not know the meaning of *cow* if we did not know all the cows in the world. This is why a 'naming' approach to meaning is bound to be unsuccessful (2.1).

Failure to make the distinction can lead to paradoxes. It is at the centre of the problem concerning *the morning star* and *the evening star*. How could it ever have been that people did not know that the morning star was the evening star? For this would seem to suggest that they did not know that Venus was Venus. The point, of course, is that the extension of these two expressions is the same (Venus), but their intensions are different (though, in fact, the description is inaccurate since Venus is a planet, not a star). Without knowing the correct extensions of the expressions, it was perfectly possible for people not to know that the morning star and the evening star were the same. Similarly, Carnap (1948: 24) pointed out that *featherless biped* and *rational animal* have the same extensions (human beings), but clearly different intensions.

The point is even more striking for expressions that have intensions but not extensions, e.g. *the women who have walked on the moon* and *the cats who are professional footballers*. Their extensions are the same – the null set, though clearly their intensions are different. It is also clear that we should not want to say that they have the same meaning.

Logicians are not, however, usually concerned with the actual world but with POSSIBLE WORLDS. A possible world must not be thought of as some other inhabited planet existing in some other galaxy or as a creation of a science fiction writer, but rather as a state of affairs which may be different from the state of affairs, the world, that we experience (or it may not be different, since 'our' world is, in this sense, one possible world). There are two reasons for doing this. The first is that the logician, and indeed the linguist, is not primarily concerned with practical questions such as 'What does this word/sentence mean?', but with theoretical questions about what it is for a word or sentence to have a meaning. It is not directly relevant, therefore, what the world is actually like. More importantly, perhaps, we often talk about different 'worlds', in the sense that we envisage that things could be different from what they are. This is clear enough in conditional sentences and wishes such as *If I had lived in Egypt, I would have spoken Arabic* and *I wish I spoke Arabic*. The world of belief, too, is different from the actual world. Possible worlds are also involved in epistemic and deontic modality (6.8), and, indeed, logicians have used the term MODAL LOGIC to refer to analysis in terms of possible worlds, though clearly this is to use the term *modal* in a much wider sense.

There are some ambiguities and problems that can be dealt with in terms of extensions and intensions and of the notion of possible worlds (the literature on the subject is very large, but is not altogether clear or consistent).

We may note, to begin with, the distinction made by Donnellan (1966 [1971: 102ff.]) between the REFERENTIAL and the ATTRIBUTIVE uses of referential expressions. He points out that *Smith's murderer is insane* is ambiguous, since it may mean either that a certain person, e.g. Jones, who is known to have murdered Smith, is insane, or that the person who murdered Smith, whoever he may be (and it may not be known who he is), is insane. In the first case (the referential use), the expression *Smith's murderer* is being used to identify someone and is thus concerned with extension in the real world; in the second case (the attributive use), we are more concerned with the description itself, with the intension of the expression and with its extension only in possible worlds.

Secondly, we may notice the ambiguity in the sentence *Mary believes that the President is handsome*. Although one man, e.g. Mr Smith, may, in fact, be President, Mary may believe that someone else, e.g. Mr Brown, is the President; the sentence may thus be taken to mean either that she believes that Mr Smith is handsome or that she believes that Mr Brown is handsome. This kind of ambiguity is usually handled in terms of a *de re* and a *de dicto* interpretation ('about the thing' and 'about what is said' – cf. Allwood et al. 1977: 114–15, who offer the example *John believes the man who robbed him was red-haired*). In the one case we are concerned with the man who actually is President, and in the other with the man who is said, or believed, to be President. What seems to be at issue here is the extension of *the President* – either Mr Smith in the real world, or Mr Brown in the world of Mary's belief.

Closely associated with this is what have been called OPAQUE contexts (cf. Quine 1960: 141ff.). Consider a situation in which Professor Green is the Dean. Then it will not necessarily follow that, if *John believes that Professor Green is a genius* is true, *John believes that the Dean is a genius* is also true, even though *The Dean is tall* will be true if *Professor Green is tall* is true. For obviously, if John does not know that Professor Green is the Dean, he may believe that Professor Green is a genius, without necessarily believing that the Dean is a genius. An opaque context is defined as one in which truth is not preserved when certain types of co-referential expressions are substituted for one another. Thus, since Professor Green and the Dean are the same person, *Professor Green* and *the Dean* are co-referential expressions, but they cannot be substituted in the first pair of sentences with truth preservation. The same arguments can be applied to the examples *the morning star* and *the evening star* since *Copernicus knew that the morning star was a planet* and *Copernicus knew that the evening star was a planet* would not both be true or both false if Copernicus did not know that the morning star and the evening star were the same (Allwood et al. 1977: 119).

It may be noted that there is (at least) triple ambiguity in *John believes that Smith's murderer is insane*. For *Smith's murderer* may be taken to refer to Jones, who actually murdered Smith, or to someone else, e.g. Black, who John believes to have murdered Smith (with the same ambiguity as that of *the President*), or, in the attributive sense, to 'whoever it may be that murdered Smith'. Both the attributive/referential distinction and that of *de re/de dicto* are (independently) involved here.

There is, however, also ambiguity in *Bill is looking for the Dean*, since this means either that Bill is looking for Professor Green who is, in fact, the Dean, or that he is looking for the person, whoever it may be, who is Dean. It would appear that this is a matter of the attributive and referential use of the expression *the Dean*. Nevertheless, it may not be irrelevant that *look for* also seems to provide opaque contexts. It may be argued that, if, for instance, the Dean is also the Professor of History, so that *the Dean* and *the Professor of History* are co-referential, it is not necessarily the case that *Bill is looking for the Dean* entails *Bill is looking for the Professor of History* (cf. Quine 1960: 142).

With expressions like *look for*, however, there is a very similar ambiguity when we have INDEFINITE rather than DEFINITE expressions. (Definite expressions identify specific individuals, usually with the definite article *the* or by proper names – though *Smith's murderer* is also a definite expression with the meaning 'THE murderer of Smith'; indefinite expressions are usually introduced by the indefinite article *a*.) Thus *I am looking for a pencil* may mean either that I am looking for a particular pencil or that any pencil will do. The difference here is usually treated in linguistics in terms of the SPECIFIC and NON-SPECIFIC use of the indefinite expressions. The close parallelism with *Bill is looking for the Dean* is obvious; in the first sense we are looking for a particular object that happens to be a pencil, while in the second we are looking for anything that fits the description. However, it is not certain whether we can identify the specific/non-specific distinction with that of referential/attributive. In particular, the specific/non-specific distinction seems to be clearly made only in opaque contexts. For, whereas the ambiguity of *Smith's murderer is insane* (with a definite noun phrase) is obvious, it is at least debatable whether there is exactly the same ambiguity in e.g. *Someone is conservative* (i.e. either that some specific person known to the speaker is conservative, or that at least one person is conservative – see Allwood et al. 1977: 116), or in *Someone is asking for trouble*, where it may, or may not be, clear who the 'someone' is.

There is a similar, perhaps identical, ambiguity in *John wants to marry a girl with green eyes* (Lyons 1977: 190–1) and *John must talk to someone* (Allwood et al. 1977: 116). On the specific readings there is a particular girl with green eyes that John wants to marry and a particular person that he must talk to. On the non-specific readings he has no specific girl in mind, but merely requires that his future wife has green eyes, while it does not matter who it is that he talks to, as long as he talks to someone. There would seem to be some similarity between *John must talk to someone* and *Everyone loves someone*. The ambiguity of the latter can be dealt with in terms of scope – $\forall x \, \exists y \, (L(x,y))$ vs. $\exists y \, \forall x \, (L(x,y))$. It has been suggested that if we treat *must* as the 'modal operator' O, we can show the ambiguity in exactly the same way, in terms of the order of $\exists$ and O: $O \, \exists x \, (T(a,x))$ vs. $\exists x \, O \, (T(a,x))$. In the first the 'existence of someone' falls under the scope of 'must', whereas in the second it is independent of it, so that, while in the first it is necessary for someone to exist, and he exists only in the 'modal' world, in the second he exists independently of the necessity – in the real world. But such an analysis is less plausible with our 'girl with green eyes' example, while its application to definite expressions involves a complicated formalism that disguises the similarity between all the examples we have been considering (Allwood et al. 1977: 156–7), and, in any case, it is not at all obvious that we should deal with all the problems and ambiguities in the same way – in terms of scope.

8.5 *Truth-conditional semantics*

The logical analyses presented in 8.3 and 8.4 took no account

of what we would normally regard as the meaning of the
sentences we were considering, but only their truth or falsity
and their logical form. It seems only natural that an attempt
should be made to extend the techniques of the logical calculi
to deal also with what it is that sentences 'mean'. One such
attempt is what has been called FORMAL SEMANTICS or TRUTH-
CONDITIONAL SEMANTICS (though it is a little unfortunate that
the term *formal* should be used in yet another sense, to refer
to the abstract 'formal' languages of logic).

This shares with the logical calculi the basic assumption
that sentences (or propositions – see below) are either true or
false, but their truth or falsity is relative to the world (or a
possible world). This, moreover, is seen as a matter of meaning or semantics, since, it is claimed, to know the meaning of
a sentence is to know the conditions under which it is (or
would be) true. It is, however, not suggested that this will
capture all that we would normally mean by 'meaning', and
for that reason a distinction is made between SEMANTICS and
PRAGMATICS (cf. Morris 1938: 6; Carnap 1948: 9), such that
only what can be handled in terms of truth and falsity ('truth
conditionality') is a matter of semantics. All the rest, and
especially all the judgments that speakers make in their
decisions about what to say and when to say it, are matters of
pragmatics.

The starting point for the argument that to know the
meaning of a sentence is to know the conditions under which
a sentence is true is usually Tarski's (1936 [1956: 155])
definition – 'a true sentence is one which states that the state
of affairs is so and so, and the state of affairs is so and so'. This
is often discussed (Kempson 1977: 24; Lyons 1977: 168) with
the example:

> *'Snow is white' if and only if snow is white.*

In fact, Tarski proposed this as the basis of a theory of truth,
but it is easy to see how it can be converted into a theory of
meaning. At first glance this dictum may seem to be completely uninformative. Of course snow is white if snow is

white! But that misses the point of what is being suggested. For the dictum makes sense only if we clearly distinguish between the sentence that we are talking about (here represented in quotation marks), which is part of the OBJECT LANGUAGE, and what we are saying about it (that it is true under certain conditions), which is part of the META-LANGUAGE. Thus we match a bit of language with a set of conditions in the world, and it does not matter if the words *snow is white* appear in both, for both the object language and the metalanguage are, in this case, English. But we could well have used another language as the metalanguage, or even a set of logical formulae.

More importantly, there would be very little point in the exercise if we were merely to take each individual sentence and state the individual set of conditions under which it is true. What we have to do (as in other areas of linguistics) is reduce the problem to the analysis of a small number of simple sentences with simple truth conditions, and then write rules that will account for the more complex sentences of the language and their more complex sets of truth conditions. Thus, to put it very simply, the meaning of *John loves Mary* can be stated in terms of the condition that there are two individuals in the world identified as John and Mary such that there is a relationship of loving between them. The meaning of the more complex sentence *Harry believes that John loves Mary* would be given by showing, first, the rules by which it can be constructed from simple sentences, and, secondly, how its truth conditions are determined by these rules.

The assumption in the last paragraph is that we can state truth conditions in terms of individuals, things, events, states of affairs, etc., in the world. But that is to deal with them in terms of their extensions. Might it not be easier to deal with them in terms of their intensions? Let us consider tentatively, very briefly (and, perhaps, a little naively) how this might be done.

In 8.4 we dealt only with the intensions and extensions of

nominal expressions such as *the Dean*, *the man who robbed him*. Informally, intensions can be seen as the set of properties they indicate, and the extensions the set of entities to which they refer in the actual (or a possible) world (cf. Carnap 1956: 19). Thus, the intension of *cow* is the property 'bovine' and its extension (in the actual world) the set of all cows in the world. More strictly, intensions are defined as 'functions from possible worlds into extensions'. The intension of an expression, that is to say, is precisely what it is that allows us to 'pick out' the extension of that expression in any possible world. The distinction can now be extended to sentences. The extension of a sentence can be seen as the state of affairs, etc., to which it refers. What then is its intension? The usual answer is 'a proposition'. For just as we must match the intension of *cow* ('bovine') with its extension (all the cows in the world), so we must match the intension of a sentence (the proposition it expresses) with all those states of affairs to which it may refer in any possible world.

We can now think of the world or any possible world as an intensional world, as a set of propositions, rather than a state of affairs. This has some obvious advantages. First, it enables us to avoid the question of what the world of experience is actually like – what are the entities in it, what are the states of affairs; instead we have what are essentially descriptions that we can, in principle at least, match with this extensional world. Secondly, we can state logical relations between propositions and, in particular, we may make use of the concepts 'true' and 'false'. For each proposition may be true or false, may be regarded as either being or not being IN that intensional world. Thus the proposition expressed by *Pigs can fly* is not in (or not true in) the actual world, but is in the hypothetical world of *If pigs could fly* . . . Propositions are, however, normally stated in terms of predication – of individuals and predicates, as would be shown for the formula for *Pigs fly* $\forall x \ (P(x) \rightarrow F(x))$, where both P ('being a pig') and F ('fly') are predicated of the individuals. This will pick out, in the extensional world, the entities that are pigs and those that fly, plus the fact that the latter set includes the former.

As we have already seen (8.4), a statement in propositional terms will often resolve some ambiguities that are found in ordinary language and cannot be resolved by any clearly grammatical analysis. We need this disambiguation before we can state the truth conditions of such sentences. We shall, for instance, need two different sets of truth conditions for *Everyone loves someone*. It does not, however, follow that traditional-type predicate calculus will be used. One of its problems is that it provides very different analyses for what seems to be similar phenomena. But we need some kind of 'disambiguated' language.

A linguistic model along these lines will have five levels or components: (1) the language itself, (2) the grammatical description of that language, (3) the disambiguated ('logical') language, (4) the intensional world of propositions, (5) the extensional world.

One of the best known types of truth-conditional semantics is 'Montague grammar' (for an account see Partee 1975). The two components of this are its 'syntax' and 'semantics', but these correspond roughly only to (3) and (4). The syntax has relatively little to say about syntax in the usual grammatical sense (although it uses a descriptive model that has been mostly used for grammatical syntax), but is essentially a disambiguated language, and one, moreover, that attempts to treat in similar ways some sentences that predicate logic treats very differently. We find, for instance, similar structures for *Every man loves a woman* and *John seeks a unicorn*. This allows easier access to the semantics which is in terms of the truth conditions that are associated with the formulae of the syntax.

Much of the work in truth-conditional semantics is of a highly technical nature, and it may be argued that it cannot rightly be evaluated without a detailed exposition. But the linguist can only have serious doubts about its value for him if he thinks that semantics should, at least in a minimal way, tell him something about the relation between his language and the world of experience. Moreover, he may well expect this to be the case in view of the talk about 'state of affairs', 'truth conditions', etc. But he is likely to be disappointed. To begin with, the idea of an intensional world that consists of a set of propositions seems rather unhelpful, if we do not see how precisely this may be related to our 'real' extensional world. The definition of intension in terms of what it is that allows us to 'pick out' extensions seems to beg all the important questions, for, surely, we need to have a clear idea of what the world is like before we can attempt to give it an intensional description. But he may be even more disappointed when he finds that the logician's extensional world, too, is not really at all like his world of experience, but is essentially yet another abstract system. For, as Carnap (1956: 21, 145ff.) argued, although it may be useful to talk about extensions and intensions, classes and properties, they are really different ways of looking at the same things; we can, if we try, produce a language that is quite neutral between these two ways of speaking. But, if this is so, we have not left the realm of formal languages, and the question of the relevance of either an intensional or an extensional description to natural language or to the world of experience is still quite open. Secondly, as we noted before, language is not merely, or even primarily, a matter of making statements. Yet it is by no means certain that these formal languages can deal satisfactorily with questions and commands. Thirdly, whether we have an intensional description in terms of individual concepts and their properties, or an extensional description in terms of individuals and the classes to which they belong, this is a rather curious way of looking at language and experience. For the entire description will be in terms of the relations between sets of e.g. flying things and pigs (or of the intensional concepts that have the relevant properties). Such an analysis will even have to be provided for *John walks*, *John loves Mary* or even *John hopes that Mary will be better tomorrow*.

This is not to say there is no value in the discussions. The notion of a disambiguated language is useful as is the distinction between intension and extension in the solution of the problems we discussed. But the usefulness is limited. The problem with formal languages is that they derive their validity from their own internal consistency, coherence and elegance and not from their applicability to real problems.

8.6 *Truth conditions and linguistics*

In the last section we were discussing what was essentially a philosophical issue that has no direct bearing upon the way in which we use language to express meaning (except where the problems of disambiguation were raised). But truth-conditional semantics has been proposed as a way of dealing with some of the linguistic issues that we have already encountered.

It will be recalled that a truth-conditional account of presupposition has been suggested (7.4, 8.2). It may also be possible to deal with implicatures (7.5) in the same way. Smith & Wilson (1979: 149–50, 172–3) consider the situation in which it is known that either Barbara Cartland or Patrick White is going to win the Literature Prize; *It won't be Patrick White* will then convey the information that Barbara Cartland will win it. Now it is obvious that, if we think of the shared knowledge as the proposition *Either Barbara Cartland or Patrick White will win the prize* and the utterance as *Patrick White will not win the prize* we can draw the logical conclusion *Barbara Cartland will win the prize*. Not all implicatures will be as simple as this. For instance, the reply to *Where's my box of chocolates?* may be *I was feeling hungry*, from which it can be inferred that they have all gone; this involves the shared knowledge about what people do when they are hungry, why questions are not answered directly, etc. In principle both the meaning of the reply and all the shared knowledge could be stated in propositional terms and, if so, the conclusion could be drawn in a logical way. This would seem to be a reasonable interpretation of the suggestion that we need only the maxim of relation to account for implicatures and that relevance may be defined in terms of 'A remark P is relevant to another remark Q, if P and Q, together with background knowledge, yield new information not derivable from either P or Q, together with background knowledge, alone' (Smith & Wilson 1979: 177). 'Remarks', 'background knowledge' and 'new information' can all, in theory, be treated as propositions or sets of propositions.

There are, however, difficulties with such analysis, involving the status of the 'background knowledge'. For it is by no means certain that this can be stated in propositional terms, and, if it cannot, it is difficult to see how new information can be derived. Thus to say that I know that it is raining is not the same thing as to say that the proposition *It is raining* is part of my knowledge. For my dog may know that it is raining, but it seems unreasonable to suggest that he entertains propositions. Secondly, this knowledge is private and not directly accessible to the observer, and there is therefore a grave danger that if the investigator is not himself the speaker he may be involved in circular reasoning. For although he may wish to predict the conclusion (the implicature) from the relevant propositions, he will often be unable to establish what are the propositions in the 'background knowledge' except from the implicature that is drawn.

Let us take another example. It has been suggested that *John has a yacht* may implicate that John is rich (Kempson 1975: 160; cf. Lakoff 1971: 130), but it has been pointed out that, if this had been said by a very rich man who owned an ocean-going cruiser, it might implicate that John was relatively poor. So the speaker might continue with either *So we can ask him to contribute* or *So we can't ask him to contribute*. In one case the background information would contain the proposition *All yacht owners are rich*; in the other *All yacht owners are poor*. But we cannot establish what these propositions are without reference to the conclusion; it would then be circular to account for the conclusion in terms of the proposition.

Of more direct linguistic relevance is the proposal (Kempson 1977: 38ff.; cf. Wilson 1975: 5) that the relations between such words as *bachelor* and *unmarried, male, human, adult* can be handled in truth-conditional terms. For the truth conditions for *John is a bachelor* are included in the conditions for *John is unmarried, John is male, John is human* and *John is adult*, and we can say that *John is a bachelor* entails these other sentences. Now it had been argued (Quine 1951 [1953: 22–3]; cf. Carnap 1956: 223) that the sentences *No unmarried man is married* and *No bachelor is married* are alike, in that their truth does not depend upon facts about the world. They are ANALYTIC statements, as opposed to SYNTHETIC ones, whose truth is dependent on such facts. But only sentences of the first kind involve logical truth. Carnap went on to propose that, in order to handle such sentences as the second, we need meaning postulates (5.2) like $\forall x \ (B(x) \rightarrow \sim M(x))$ 'for all *x*s, *x* is a bachelor implies *x* is not married'. But it should be clear from this that, when it is said that *John is a bachelor* entails *John is unmarried*, 'entails' is not being used in the sense of material implication (8.2) which is a matter of logical truth. Material implication simply relates sentences in terms of their truth value, and any true sentence implies any other true sentence. Thus *John is a bachelor* may imply *John is a bus-conductor*. What we have here can only be strict implication, which involves 'truth in all possible worlds'. To say that *John is a bachelor* entails *John is unmarried* is to say that in all possible worlds, if the first is true, the second is true.

It should be noted, however, that a number of philosophers have argued (e.g. Bar-Hillel 1970: 206–21) that analytic statements of this kind (restricting the term 'analytic' to those that do not involve logical truth) should be thought to be matters not of semantics, but of pragmatics, since they depend upon conventions accepted by the speakers of the language. What we have here is pragmatic, not semantic, implication.

The chief difficulty for any truth-conditional treatment is the problem of the relation between analytic and synthetic statements. For we can, it would seem, distinguish between what is necessarily true and what contingently true (because of facts in the world). Thus we may compare:

> *All bachelors are unmarried.*
> *All bachelors are happy.*

The first is an analytic truth that does not depend upon our knowledge of the world, but the truth (or falsity) of the second is synthetic, and can only be proved by observation. The relevance of possible worlds is clear. An analytic truth is true in all worlds: in no possible world could a bachelor be married. A synthetic truth is true only in this world and certain others: even if it is true that bachelors are happy, it is certainly not true of all conceivable worlds.

Unfortunately, language is not as tidy as this might suggest. The relation between words is not always as well-defined as that between *bachelor* and *unmarried*. For consider:

> *All misers are stingy.*
> *All misers are rich.*
> *All misers are miserable.*

Which of these are analytic and which synthetic? To answer that we must know whether the definition of *miser* includes 'being stingy', 'being rich' and 'being miserable'. Generally we might feel certain about the first, but less than certain about the other two. Consider, similarly, *All birds have two legs*, *All birds have feathers*, *All birds fly*, *All birds sing*. The last two are almost certainly synthetically false, but the status of the others is in some doubt.

The problem is no less obvious with:

> *All carnivores eat meat.*
> *All mammals produce live young.*

It might be thought that these are analytically true, that it is part of the definition of carnivore that it eats meat, that it is part of the definition of mammal that it produces live young.

However, the giant panda, which is classified by zoologists as a carnivore, lives almost exclusively on bamboo shoots, while the platypus, which is classified as a mammal, lays eggs. In the light of this the sentences above are not analytically true, and are, moreover, synthetically false. Of course, we can redefine *carnivore* and *mammal* to exclude the panda and the platypus and retain the analytic truth. But whether we are involved in an analytic or a synthetic judgment depends on the definition of *carnivore* and *mammal*. The scientist is perfectly entitled to modify his definitions to ensure that they are watertight. If he comes across a new plant, or a creature that seems to invalidate his definitions, he can change them. For instance, the characteristic of meat-eating could well have been included in the original definition of carnivore, but dropped when the giant panda was found, since this creature has other characteristics of carnivores but does not eat meat. Thus by dropping the most 'obvious' characteristic the scientist would have been able to preserve the rest of his classificatory system.

The scientist, then, can decide to make his definitions in such a way that he knows whether a sentence is analytically or synthetically true. But ordinary speakers of a language cannot do this, for the definition of a word is not within the individual's power. We may, then, be faced with problems of the kind 'When is a stool not a stool?' For I am not at all sure whether *This stool has a broken back* is anomalous (Is part of the definition of stool that it has no back?), or whether *All pies have pastry on top* is analytically true (Is part of the definition of *pie* that it has a top?). When we turn to sets of nouns such as *chair, armchair, settee, couch, divan, chaise-longue*, etc., we shall find ourselves in numerous problems of this kind. It is not at all clear whether 'armchair without arms' is a contradiction in terms since the 'lady's chair' in a suite used to be larger than the rest (except the 'gentleman's chair'), but it had no arms. With verbs the problems are even more difficult. Can a man *trot* at fifteen miles an hour or take *strides* of eighteen inches? The answers are not at all certain, yet the decision whether a sentence is or is not anomalous will depend upon such answers.

In practice there is no difficulty. The problem of analytic/ synthetic does not prevent us from communicating or from writing dictionaries. But the fact that there are these problems shows how unsatisfactory a truth-conditional treatment of the lexicon will be. At best it will deal with only a fraction of the relations that hold between lexical items, and even then will claim for them a precision that they do not have. That should not, of course, deter us from stating the relations and, where we can, presenting them in an organised and simplified form. This is, of course, precisely what we attempted to do in the treatment of sense relations in Chapter 5.

8.7 *Concluding remarks*

One conclusion that will be drawn from reading this book is that semantics is not a single, well-integrated discipline. It is not a clearly defined level of linguistics, not even comparable to phonology or grammar. Rather it is a set of studies of the use of language in relation to many different aspects of experience, to linguistic and non-linguistic context, to participants in discourse, to their knowledge and experience, to the conditions under which a particular bit of language is appropriate. Indeed there is a sense in which, as we have seen, semantics relates to the sum total of human knowledge, though it must be the task of the linguist to limit the field of his study and bring order to the apparent confusion and complexity.

It would be foolhardy to attempt to forecast precisely what future trends will be. Some linguists are concentrating upon formal semantics, while others would argue that semantics should not simply be concerned with formal, semi-logical systems within language, but is more a matter of relating language to the world of experience; and within the wider discipline of linguistics there has been some shift of interest away from 'pure' theory to such topics as sociolinguistics (the study of the role of language in society) and the acquisition of language by children.

Yet we must accept the fact that there will be no 'massive breakthrough'. The complexity of semantics is merely one aspect of the complexity of human language. What we can say will be unprecise and often controversial. There are no easy answers.

REFERENCES

Allwood, J., Anderson, L-G & Dähl, Ö. 1977. *Logic in linguistics*. Cambridge: Cambridge University Press.

Austin, J. L. 1962. *How to do things with words*. London: Oxford University Press.

Bach, E. & Harms, R. J. (eds.) 1968. *Universals in linguistic theory*. New York: Holt, Rinehart & Winston.

Bar-Hillel, Y. 1970. *Aspects of language*. Jerusalem: Magnes.

Bazell, C. E. 1954. 'The sememe'. *Litera* 1, 17–31. Reprinted in Hamp et al. 1966: 329–40.

Berlin, B. & Kay, P. 1969. *Basic color terms*. Berkeley & Los Angeles: University of California Press.

Bierwisch, M. 1970. 'Semantics'. In Lyons 1970: 166–84.

Bloomfield, L. 1926. 'A set of postulates for the science of language'. *Language* 2, 153–164. Reprinted in Joos 1958: 26–31.

1933. *Language*. New York: Holt, and (1935) London: Allen & Unwin.

Boas, F. 1911. *Introduction to the Handbook of American Indian languages*. Washington, DC. Reprinted (no date) by Georgetown University Press.

Bréal, M. 1900. *Semantics: studies in the science of meaning*. London: Heinemann.

Brown, R. & Gilman, A. 1960. 'The pronouns of power and solidarity'. In Sebeok 1960: 253–76.

Carnap, R. 1937. *The logical syntax of language*. London: Kegan Paul.

1948. *Introduction to semantics*. Cambridge, Mass.: Harvard University Press.

1956. *Meaning and necessity*. Chicago: Chicago University Press.

Chomsky, N. 1957. *Syntactic structures*. The Hague: Mouton.

1959. Review of B. F. Skinner 1957. *Language* 35, 26–57. Reprinted in Fodor & Katz 1964: 547–78.

1965. *Aspects of the theory of syntax*. Cambridge, Mass.: MIT Press.

1970. 'Remarks on nominalization'. In Jacobs & Rosenbaum 1970: 184–221.

1971. 'Deep structure, surface structure and semantic interpretation'. In Steinberg & Jakobovits 1971: 183–216.

1977. *Essays in form and interpretation*. Amsterdam: North Holland.

Cole, P. & Morgan, J. L. (eds.) 1975. *Syntax and semantics, 3. Speech acts.* New York & London: Academic Press.

Cole, P. & Sadock, J. M. (eds.) 1977. *Syntax and semantics, 8. Grammatical relations.* New York & London: Academic Press.

Conklin, H. C. 1955. 'Hanunóo Color'. *Southwestern Journal of Anthropology* 11, 339–44. Reprinted in Hymes 1964: 189–91.

Crystal, D. 1969. *Prosodic systems and intonation in English.* Cambridge: Cambridge University Press.

Crystal, D. & Davy, D. 1969. *Investigating English style.* London: Longman.

Daneš, F. 1968. 'Some thoughts on the semantic structure of the sentence'. *Lingua* 21, 55–9.

Donnellan, K. 1966. 'Reference and definite descriptions'. *Philosophical Review* 75, 281–304. Reprinted in Steinberg & Jakobovits 1971: 100–14.

Ferguson, C. A. 1959. 'Diglossia'. *Word* 15, 325–40. Reprinted in Hymes 1964: 429–39.

Fillmore, C. J. 1966. 'Deictic categories in the semantics of "come"'. *Foundations of Language* 2, 219–27.

1968. 'The case for case'. In Bach & Harms 1968: 1–90.

1971a. 'Types of lexical information'. In Steinberg & Jakobovits 1971: 370–92.

1971b. 'Verbs of judging: an exercise in semantic description'. In Fillmore & Langendoen 1971: 273–89.

1977. 'The case for case reopened'. In Cole & Sadock 1977: 59–81.

Fillmore, C. J. & Langendoen, D. T. (eds.) 1971. *Studies in linguistic semantics.* New York: Holt, Rinehart & Winston.

Firbas, J. 1959. 'Thoughts on the communicative function of the verb in English'. *Brno Studies in English* 1, 39–68.

1964. 'On defining theme in functional sentence analysis'. *Travaux linguistiques de Prague* 1, 267–80.

Firth, J. R. 1950. 'Personality and language in society'. *The Sociological Review* 42, 37–52. Reprinted in Firth 1957a: 177–89.

1951. 'Modes of meaning'. *Essays and Studies (The English Association),* 118–49. Reprinted in Firth 1957a: 190–215.

1957a. *Papers in Linguistics 1934–1951.* London: Oxford University Press.

1957b. 'A synopsis of linguistic theory 1930–1955'. *Studies in linguistic analysis* (Special volume of the Philological Society), 1–32. Oxford: Blackwell. Reprinted in Firth 1968: 168–205.

1968. *Selected papers of J. R. Firth 1952–1959,* ed. F. R. Palmer. London: Longman, and Bloomington: Indiana University Press.

Fishman, J. A. 1970. *Sociolinguistics.* Rowley, Mass.: Newbury House.

Fodor, J. A. & Katz, J. J. 1964. *The structure of language: readings in the philosophy of language.* New Jersey: Prentice-Hall.

Fries, C. C. 1952. *The structure of English*. New York: Harcourt Brace, and (1957) London: Longman.

Grice, H. P. 1975. 'Logic and conversation'. In Cole & Morgan 1975: 41–58.

Haas, W. 1973. 'Meanings and rules'. *Proceedings of the Aristotelian Society 1972–3*, 126–55.

Hall, R. A. 1964. *Introductory linguistics*. Philadelphia & New York: Chilton Books.

Halliday, M. A. K. 1970. 'Language structure and language function'. In Lyons 1970: 140–65.

Hamp, E. P., Householder, F. W. & Austerlitz, R.(eds.) 1966. *Readings in linguistics II*. London & Chicago: Chicago University Press.

Hjelmslev, L. 1953. 'Prolegomena to a theory of language' (translated by F. J. Whitfield). *International Journal of American Linguistics* Memoir 7.

Hockett, C. F. 1958. *A course in modern linguistics*. New York: Macmillan.

Hymes, D. (ed.) 1964. *Language in culture and society*. New York: Harper & Row.

Jackendoff, R. S. 1969. 'An interpretive theory of negation'. *Foundations of Language* 5, 218–41.

  1972. *Semantic interpretation in generative grammar*. Cambridge, Mass.: MIT Press.

Jacobs, R. A. & Rosenbaum, P. S. (eds.) 1970. *Readings in English transformational grammar*. Waltham, Mass.: Ginn & Co.

Johnson, D. E. 1974. 'On the role of grammatical relations in linguistic theory'. *Papers from the Tenth Regional Meeting, Chicago Linguistics Society*, 269–83.

Joos, M. 1950. 'Description of language design'. *Journal of the Acoustical Society of America* 22, 701–8. In Joos 1958: 329–56.

  (ed.) 1958. *Readings in linguistics*. New York: American Council of Learned Societies.

  1962. *The five clocks*. (Publications of the Indiana University Research Center in Anthropology, Folklore and Linguistics, 22.) Bloomington: Indiana University, and The Hague: Mouton.

  1964. *The English verb: form and meaning*. Madison: University of Wisconsin Press.

Katz, J. J. 1966. *The philosophy of language*. New York: Harper & Row. Partly reprinted in Steinberg & Jakobovits 1971: 297–307.

  1972. *Semantic theory*. New York: Harper & Row.

Katz, J. J. & Fodor, J. A. 1963. 'The structure of a semantic theory'. *Language* 39, 170–210. Reprinted in Fodor & Katz, 1964: 479–518.

Katz, J. J. & Postal, P. M. 1964. *An integrated theory of linguistic descriptions*. Cambridge, Mass.: MIT Press.

Kay, P. 1975. 'Synchronic variability and diachronic change in basic color terms'. *Language in Society* 4, 257–70.

Keenan, E. L. 1971. 'Two kinds of presupposition'. In Fillmore & Langendoen 1971: 45–54.

Kempson, R. M. 1975. *Presupposition and the delimitation of semantics*. Cambridge: Cambridge University Press.

1977. *Semantic theory*. Cambridge: Cambridge University Press.

Kiparsky, P. & Kiparsky, C. 1971. 'Fact'. In Steinberg & Jakobovits 1971: 345–69.

Lakoff, G. 1968. 'Instrumental adverbs and the concept of deep structure'. *Foundations of Language* 4, 4–29.

1971a. 'On generative semantics'. In Steinberg & Jakobovits 1971: 232–96.

1971b. 'Presupposition and relative grammaticality'. In Steinberg & Jakobovits 1971: 329–40.

1971c. 'The role of deduction in grammar'. In Fillmore & Langendoen 1971: 63–72.

Lakoff, R. 1971. '"Ifs" "ands" and "buts" about conjunction'. In Fillmore & Langendoen 1971: 115–50.

Lounsbury, F. G. 1956. 'A semantic analysis of Pawnee kinship usage'. *Language* 32, 158–194.

Lyons, J. 1963. *Structural semantics*. Oxford: Blackwell.

1968. *Introduction to theoretical linguistics*. Cambridge: Cambridge University Press.

(ed.) 1970. *New horizons in linguistics*. Harmondsworth, Middlesex: Penguin Books.

1977. *Semantics*. (2 vols.) Cambridge: Cambridge University Press.

McIntosh, A. 1961. 'Patterns and ranges'. *Language* 37, 325–37.

McNeill, N. B. 1972. 'Colour and colour terminology'. *Journal of Linguistics* 8, 21–34.

Malinowski, B. 1923. *The problem of meaning in primitive languages*. Supplement to Ogden & Richards 1923 (tenth edition 1949).

Matthews, G. H. 1965. *Hidatsa syntax*. The Hague: Mouton.

Morgan, J. L. 1969. 'On arguing about semantics'. *Papers in Linguistics* 1, 49–70.

Morris, C. W. 1938. 'Foundations of the theory of signs'. In Neurath, Carnap & Morris 1938: 79–137.

1946. *Signs, language and behavior*. New York: Prentice-Hall.

Neurath, O., Carnap, R. & Morris, C. W. (eds.) 1938. *International Encyclopaedia of Unified Sciences*. (Combined edition 1955.) Chicago: University of Chicago Press.

Nida, E. A. 1964. *Towards a science of translating*. Leiden: Brill.

O'Connor, J. D. & Arnold, G. F. 1961. *Intonation of colloquial English*. London: Longman.

Ogden, C. K. & Richards, I. A. 1923. *The meaning of meaning*. London: Kegan Paul. (Tenth edition 1949.)

Osgood, C. E. Suci, G. J. & Tannenbaum, P. H. 1957. *The measurement of meaning*. Urbana: University of Illinois Press.

Palmer, F. R. 1971. *Grammar*. Harmondsworth, Middlesex: Penguin Books.

1974. *The English verb*. London: Longman.

1979. *Modality and the English modals*. London: Longman.

Partee, B. 1975. 'Montague grammar and transformational grammar'. *Linguistic Inquiry* 6, 203–300.

Porzig, W. 1934. 'Wessenhafte Bedeutungsbeziehungen'. *Beiträge zur Geschichte der deutschen Sprache und Literatur* 58, 70–97.

Quine, W. V. O. 1951. 'Two dogmas of empiricism'. *Philosophical Review* 60, 20–43. Reprinted in Quine 1953: 20–46.

1953. *From a logical point of view*. Cambridge, Mass.: Harvard University Press. Reprinted 1961, New York: Harper Torchbooks.

1960. *Word and object*. Cambridge, Mass.: MIT Press.

Read, A. W. 1948. 'An account of the word "semantics"'. *Word* 4, 78–97.

Russell, B. 1905. 'On denoting'. *Mind* 14, 479–93.

1940. *An inquiry into meaning and truth*. London: Allen & Unwin. Reprinted 1962, Harmondsworth, Middlesex: Penguin Books.

Sapir, E. 1921. *Language*. New York: Harcourt, Brace & World.

1929. 'The status of linguistics as a science'. *Language* 5, 207–14. Reprinted in Sapir 1949: 160–6.

1944. 'Grading: a study in semantics'. *Philosophy of Science* 2, 93–116. Reprinted in Sapir 1949: 122–49.

1949. *Selected writings of Edward Sapir in language culture and personality*, ed. G. Mandelbaum. Berkeley & Los Angeles: University of California Press.

de Saussure, F. 1916. *Cours de linguistique générale*. Translated (1959) as *Course in general linguistics* by W. Baskin. New York: McGraw-Hill.

Searle, J. R. 1969. *Speech acts*. Cambridge: Cambridge University Press.

Sebeok, T. A. (ed.) 1960. *Style in language*. Cambridge, Mass.: MIT Press.

(ed.) 1966. *Current trends in linguistics III*. The Hague: Mouton.

Skinner, B. F. 1957. *Verbal behavior*. New York: Appleton-Century-Crofts.

Smith, N. & Wilson, D. 1979. *Modern linguistics: the results of Chomsky's revolution*. Harmondsworth, Middlesex: Penguin Books.

Steinberg, D. D. & Jakobovits, L. A. (eds.) 1971. *Semantics*. Cambridge: Cambridge University Press.

Strawson, P. F. 1964. 'Identifying reference and truth-values'. *Theoria* 30, 96–118. Reprinted in Steinberg & Jakobovits 1971: 86–99.

Sweet, H. 1891. *A new English grammar. Part I*. Oxford: Clarendon.

Tarski, A. 1936. 'Der Wahrheitsbegriff in den formalisierten Sprachen'. *Studia Philosophica* 1, 261–405. Translated and reprinted as 'The concept of truth in formalised languages' in Tarski 1956: 152–278.

1956. *Logic, semantics, and metamathematics*. Oxford: Clarendon.

Trier, J. 1934. 'Das sprachliche Feld. Eine Auseinandersetzung'. *Neue Jahrbücher fur Wissenschaft und Jugenbildung* **10**, 428–49.

Trudgill, P. 1974. *Sociolinguistics: an introduction*. Harmondsworth, Middlesex: Penguin Books.

Ullmann, S. 1962. *Semantics: an introduction to the study of meaning*. Oxford: Basil Blackwell.

Weinreich, U. 1966. 'Explorations in semantic theory'. In Sebeok 1966: 395–477.

Whorf, B. L. 1956. *Language, thought and reality: selected writings of Benjamin Lee Whorf*, ed. J. B. Carroll. Cambridge, Mass.: MIT Press.

Wilson, D. 1975. *Presupposition and non-truth conditional semantics*. London & New York: Academic Press.

Wittgenstein, L. 1953. *Philosophical investigations*. Oxford: Blackwell.

INDEX

Language and Linguistics
An Introduction
JOHN LYONS

A general introduction to linguistics and the study of language, intended particularly for beginning students. John Lyons provides an account of the nature of language and of the aims, methods and basic principles of linguistic theory. He then introduces in turn each of the main sub-fields of linguistics. In each of these sections he surveys and refers to the most significant current work and trends, but emphasises particularly those aspects of the discipline that seem fundamental and most likely to remain important.

Available in hard covers and as a paperback

Child Language
ALISON J. ELLIOT

The most important recent research in language acquisition is concisely surveyed in this textbook. Dr Elliot believes that the study of child language necessarily raises questions about the nature of human language, and about learning itself and its dependence on biological factors and social and linguistic environment. She finds little justification for the view that language has an independent existence for the young child, and here examines linguistic achievement within the context of the child's development in general.

Cambridge Textbooks in Linguistics

Available in hard covers and as a paperback

Syntax
P. H. MATTHEWS

This is a wide-ranging and original introduction to the basic concepts of syntax, illustrated mainly with English examples and designed in particular to fill the gap between the teaching of English grammar and of modern theoretical models. The chapters are divided thematically and cover all the main types of construction. Each ends with a detailed bibliographical survey, which includes notes on terminology and other points of difficulty. Students of linguistics, and English language generally, will find this a textbook of lasting value.

Cambridge Textbooks in Linguistics

Available in hard covers and as a paperback

CPSIA information can be obtained
at www.ICGtesting.com
Printed in the USA
FFOW01n1217280415
13019FF